Sigmund Freud

KNOWLEDGE
IN A
NUTSHELL

D1214419

Sigmund Freud

KNOWLEDGE IN A NUTSHELL

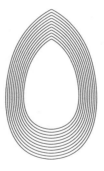

Alan Porter

ARCTURUS

ARCTURUS

This edition published in 2020 by Arcturus Publishing Limited
26/27 Bickels Yard, 151–153 Bermondsey Street,
London SE1 3HA

ISBN: 978-1-78950-221-3
AD006860UK

Printed in China

Contents

Introduction

According to Sigmund Freud's own evaluation of his life's work, he was responsible for the discovery of a method that allowed otherwise inaccessible unconscious aspects of our mental life to be revealed; he had invented an effective treatment for disorders such as hysteria and obsessive neuroses; and he was the founder of a new scientific approach to psychology. To the method, treatment and science collectively, Freud gave the name 'psychoanalysis'.

Since Freud's invention of psychoanalysis and the publication in 1900 of *The Interpretation of Dreams* (which Freud considered to be his masterpiece), his concepts of the unconscious, the Freudian slip, the id, ego and superego and a host of other terms that he introduced in his writings have become part of our common language. While our everyday understanding of these terms may not accord exactly with how Freud himself used them, it is unarguable that psychoanalysis has had a huge impact on how we think of ourselves. Many see the influence of Freud as a force for good, bringing a recognition that there are limits to our self-knowledge and encouraging us to examine what we take to be our basic motivations with care and some suspicion. Others regard his theories as having a corrosive effect, fuelling the development of a culture of self-absorption by promoting an ineffective therapy that is expensive and time-consuming, as well as encouraging reports of sexual abuse to be disbelieved and promoting a patriarchal view that defines womanhood in terms of the absence of a penis.

A portrait of Sigmund Freud taken in 1921.

The standard edition of *The Complete Psychological Works of Sigmund Freud* runs to 24 volumes. The range of Freud's work included in these volumes is considerable, from the early pre-psychoanalytic writings on hysteria to the classic accounts of dream analysis, famous case studies and a psychoanalytic biography of Leonardo da Vinci. As well as Freud's psychoanalytically related publications included in the standard edition, there are also more than a hundred papers devoted to his early work in biology and neurology, covering topics such as the search for the reproductive organs of the eel and technical papers on new methods for staining nerve cells. In addition, Freud was a great letter-writer and over the last 50 or so years his correspondence with early mentors, collaborators and students has been published, providing another source of information on how his thinking developed and changed.

The secondary literature on Freud is vast and addresses his work from psychological, political, philosophical, literary and cultural perspectives. Many biographies of Freud have been written since the first official work, *The Life and Work of Sigmund Freud* (Vols 1–3) by Ernest Jones, was published in 1953. Some of these biographies paint a picture of a genius who had to go through the pain of self-analysis to give us the gift of psychoanalysis, while others reveal a vain, dishonest and not very original thinker who has managed to hoodwink us for five generations.

In this short book it is impossible to do justice to such a huge body of work. The approach I have taken is therefore highly selective. I shall provide a guide to Freud's work by introducing his key concepts and putting them into scientific and historical context, before turning to the growth of psychoanalysis as an institution; finally, I shall address some of the criticisms that have been levelled at Freud's theories. It is inevitable that some important issues will be treated in less depth than I would like or not even discussed at all. I encourage the interested reader to turn to the primary sources and other secondary sources, treating this book as a potential map to a rich and fascinating literature. Like or loathe Freud, there is no sign that his thinking is going away.

CHAPTER I
Mind, madness and psychiatry before Freud

Over the course of his career, Freud was to invent psychoanalysis as both an all-encompassing account of the human mind and as an institution that regulated the training of professional analysts. His work was to influence academic fields including psychology, philosophy, sociology and literary theory and professional and applied fields such as psychiatry, psychotherapy and counselling. When Freud enrolled in medical school in 1873, these fields either already existed or were in the process of being formed. Freud's theories and techniques were developed in this context, and to understand where they were distinctive and where he borrowed from previous thinkers it is necessary to briefly sketch out the basic features of the scientific landscape that he was entering. The particular areas on which I shall concentrate are German Scientific Medicine, which was led by Freud's teachers; philosophical debates on the role of consciousness as a foundation for knowledge; and the rapidly changing social and medical understandings of how mental illness was to be conceptualized and treated.

THE INFLUENCE OF JOHANNES MÜLLER

By the middle of the 19th century, medicine was going through a period of rapid change. Diagnoses and treatments that had been in place for centuries were being re-examined and there was a growing tendency to use the findings of new disciplines such as physiology and biochemistry along with technologies drawn from the fields of chemistry, microscopy, physics and statistics to understand the causes of illness and devise new treatments. German science was at the heart of this movement, and *Handbuch der Physiologie des Menschen für Vorlesungen (Handbook of Physiology)* by Johannes Müller (1801–58), published in 1838, was a key text that was to influence a whole generation of biologists and medical researchers by providing them with a comprehensive and cutting-edge overview of the relationship between morphology (the study of biological structures) and physiology (the study of biological functions).

Johannes Müller was a German physiologist who had a great influence on Freud.

Hermann von Helmholtz was a physicist who made a number of discoveries in optics, physiology, electrodynamics and many other fields.

Müller surrounded himself with some of the brightest students of their generation. They included Herman Helmholtz (1821–94), Emil du Bois-Reymond (1818–96), Carl Ludwig (1816–95) and Ernst Brücke (1819–92), all of whom went on to make significant contributions to the sciences of biology and physiology. Helmholtz became one of the most renowned German scientists of the 19th century, contributing to the science of thermodynamics and formulating the principle of the conservation of force, known today as the principle of the conservation of energy. The principle states that energy cannot be created or destroyed but can only be transformed from one form to another (for example, when we switch on a lamp, electrical energy is transformed to heat and light energy).

Helmholtz also contributed to neurology by measuring the speed of nerve conduction – he measured nerve impulses travelling in frog nerves at around 27 m (88 ft) per second – and to ophthalmology, inventing the ophthalmoscope that allowed doctors to examine the interior of the eye and proposing a new theory of colour vision. Du Bois-Reymond went on to investigate the electrophysiology of nerves and muscles and Ludwig invented the kymograph, which is a device that allows physiological data such as blood pressure to be recorded over time. Brücke researched speech, the structure of skeletal muscle and plant physiology.

Clearly Johannes Müller was an innovative and original scientist who drove the agenda of scientific medicine forward. He was also a convinced vitalist, believing that the difference between a live and a dead organism was the presence or absence of a 'life energy' or, as it was sometimes called, a vital spark or *élan vital*. This vital principle was understood as a unifying force that somehow inhabited living things and left them at death. It could not be understood in terms of current physics and chemistry and, despite its description in quasi-scientific terms, was according to its critics the equivalent of the concept of 'soul' that was found in various religious traditions. Helmholtz's formulation of the principle of the conservation of energy was a direct challenge to Müller's vitalism and, although they clearly loved and respected their teacher, most of Müller's former students rejected vitalism and embraced a thorough-going materialism and reductionism, which aimed to understand the phenomena of life in terms of chemistry and physics. In 1845 Brücke, du Bois-Reymond and four other young physicists founded the *Deutsche Physikalische Gesellschaft* (German Physical Society) to promote their approach, and later that year met together to swear a solemn oath

The kymograph was invented by Carl Ludwig in 1847 and was first used to measure blood pressure.

that in their research and teaching they would explain physiological phenomena only in terms of forces that were known in, or consistent with, the laws of physics and chemistry. Brücke went on to take up appointments at Berlin and Königsberg before being appointed professor of physiology at the University of Vienna in 1849. There he kept to his oath and taught physiology as a sub-discipline of physics.

As we shall see in Chapter 2, Brücke became an important mentor to Freud, and in Chapter 3 we shall explore how Freud tried to keep to the spirit of the materialism of his teacher when he attempted to square clinical observations and neurology with the

Ernest Wilhelm von Brücke was one of Müller's most successful students, who introduced techniques from physics and chemistry into medical research.

principles of the conservation of energy and force. In 1895 Freud attempted to write this up as 'A Psychology for Neurologists' but abandoned the project as speculative, deciding instead to treat psychology, neurology and physics, in the short term at least, as separate and autonomous fields that could not as yet be connected. This work was eventually published as *Project for a Scientific Psychology* in 1950. Despite his abandonment of his reductionist programme, Freud's use of the concepts of force and energy were still to play a role in psychoanalytic thinking (see Chapter 6).

THE PRIVILEGING OF CONSCIOUSNESS

In Freud's published work there are few references to philosophy and its practitioners. However, at the University of Vienna, Freud attended lectures by Franz Clemens Brentano (1838–1917). Brentano was to influence the philosophical movement known as phenomenology, which took experience as the starting point of philosophizing rather than trying to identify the concepts that made experience possible. For Brentano the key observation when we consider our experience is that all mental acts (thinking, believing, hoping) all point beyond themselves. I might think that the sky is blue, believe that the capital of France is Paris and want a piece of cheese. These thoughts, beliefs and wants are about something and it is not so much the objects (blue skies, French seat of government and dairy products) but their very 'aboutness' that Brentano finds significant. He argues that this points to the basic difference between the mental and the physical. Mental acts all share an aboutness which is a kind of intrinsic pointing to real or imaginary targets. In contrast, purely physical things have no capacity to go beyond themselves. A rock is a rock and it is not about anything else. Brentano called this aboutness 'intentionality' and he identifies it as the mark of the mental.

In 1874 Brentano published *Psychology from an Empirical Standpoint*, in which he argued that psychology was to be the scientific study of mental phenomena and the methodology for investigating mental phenomena was introspection – that is,

Franz Brentano was a leading 19th-century philosopher who brought the idea of intentionality to the modern philosophical concepts of phenomenology.

turning the mind on itself. This was possible because, for example, when we are looking at a rock we are aware of the rock but we are also aware that we are having a thought about rock. For Brentano we can never think about the world without being aware that we are doing so. While this argument may seem rather arcane, the consequence of making the awareness of the intentionality of our mental acts the defining difference of the mental and the physical is that all mental acts are conscious acts (although the intensity of our consciousness may be very low – I may be walking along and kicking rocks from the path in front of me, but this is never a fully automatic act and at some level I am conscious that I intend to kick rocks away) and that unconscious mental acts are logically impossible. For Brentano there can be no unconscious thoughts, beliefs, feeling or hopes.

Brentano drew the distinction between the mental and the physical in terms of intentionality, but making a fundamental distinction between the mental and the physical has a much longer history. The French philosopher René Descartes (1596–1650) was highly influential in popularizing a dualist understanding of our place in the world when, more than 250 years earlier, he had attempted to put science once and for all on a solid footing by subjecting all that he knew to a process of radical doubt. His conclusion was that his only certain knowledge that was clear and distinct to his mind was the existence of his own cognitive activity of doubting. This led him to his famous statement *cogito ergo sum* – 'I think, therefore I am', which appeared in his 1644 *Principles of Philosophy*. The implications of this statement were that the very essence of a human was to be a mind – that is, a thinking, conscious being – and this knowledge of ourselves as minds was given to us with absolute certainty. Our existence as a body, along with the rest of the world, was something that could be inferred, but the starting point was our minds and there is nothing we know better than our own minds. Descartes' method of radical doubt had introduced a dualism between mind and matter – and, since our bodies are made up of matter, between mind and brain also. Descartes believed that to be a mind was to be conscious at all times, even when our bodies are in a state of sleep or when our mechanical brains are not functioning after, say, a blow to the head. In these states our minds 'withdraw' from our bodies, to return when they are in full working order. We cannot remember the conscious activity we were engaged in during these episodes of sleep or unconsciousness because no new bodily or material memories were laid down in our brains.

The upshot of Descartes' thinking is that mind is defined in terms of consciousness and that consciousness is the criterion of the mental. Just as importantly, examining our minds carefully and rejecting that which is confused or vague is the ultimate foundation for knowledge. Descartes' dualism became a guiding and dominant idea in Western philosophy, with generations of philosophers often arguing against Descartes' dualism but nevertheless using it as a starting point for further philosophizing.

Descartes himself realized that his dualism introduced problems as well as solving them. Perhaps most notably for psychologists and neurologists was working out how, if the mind and the brain are fundamentally different substances, they could ever interact. For Descartes, the site where the incorporeal and immaterial mind acted on the corporeal and material brain was via the small pineal gland situated in the middle of the brain. His argument for the importance of the pineal gland rested on it being one of the few structures in the brain that is singular; most other brain structures are mirrored in the left and right lobes of the brain. Even at the time this argument was not taken very seriously, leaving the problem of the interaction between mind and brain unsolved.

INSANITY AND THE NEUROSES

In the West there is a long and complex history of shifting conceptions of how to demarcate between sanity and insanity, the normal and the psychopathological, and the rational and the irrational. The diagnostic categories or classifications that were used to distinguish between the sane and the insane and the normal and psychopathological in the middle of the 19th century were neuroses, hysteria and mania. As we shall see in later chapters, Freud had much to say on how these distinctions should be made. Here I want merely to sketch in some background to help illuminate the medical/psychiatric/neurological field that Freud was joining when he started to train as a doctor in the 1870s.

Only 50 years before Freud's birth, asylums were filled with 'inmates' rather than 'patients' and these inmates were often treated cruelly, being considered as beyond reason, mere brutes who needed to be controlled and constrained. In the 18th and early 19th century there were some reformers such as the English philanthropist William Tuke (1732–1822), who in 1796 founded the York Retreat where patients were offered a 'moral treatment' combining gentle care with rehabilitation. Tuke embraced a compassionate understanding of 'madness', but this was the exception rather than the rule. In France, one of the most important turning points in how insanity was conceptualized and the insane were treated was instigated by Philippe Pinel (1745–1826). First at the Bicêtre Asylum in Paris and then at the Salpêtrière Hospital in the same city, Pinel famously ordered the unchaining of the patients and set about improving their living conditions, believing that acknowledging the humanity of the mad and treating them with sympathy and understanding could bring them back to reason. Freud was much taken with Pinel and described his order to remove the chains from the mad as initiating 'this most humane of revolutions'.

THE CLASSIFICATION OF MENTAL ILLNESS

As well as improving the everyday life of the patients at the Bicêtre and the Salpêtrière, Pinel concerned himself with medical classification, or nosology. The concept of nervous diseases had been in circulation since the 17th century, and the Scottish physician William Cullen (1710–90) had coined the term 'neurosis' in 1769. For Cullen, the classification of neurosis covered a very

The 16th-century French philosopher René Descartes was one of the most influential figures in the history of modern philosophy, and his idea of mind-body dualism raised important questions for psychologists.

The York Retreat was opened in 1796 to treat patients with mental health issues.

wide range of symptoms from the very serious, including melan-cholia, mania, dementia, stroke and paralysis, to the less serious, such as palpitations and colic. Among the conditions that Cullen categorized as neuroses were diarrhoea and diabetes, symptoms that today are unlikely to be considered as psychiatric disorders. Cullen believed that these diverse conditions were the result of a disordered action of the nervous system or a spasm resulting in disordered functioning. Pinel translated Cullen's work into French and, drawing on Cullen's nosology, identified five 'primi-tive' diseases comprising fever, phlegmasia (inflammation), hae-morrhage (bleeding), organic lesion and neurosis. The neuroses were defined in terms of alterations of 'sense' and 'movement' and he proposed that they should be divided into melancholia, mania without delirium, mania with delirium, dementia and idiotism.

Pinel began to move away from Cullen's understanding of neuroses as a result of systemic physiological disturbances and embraced what became known as the anatamo-clinical approach, which seeks to identify well-defined classes of symptoms with specific lesions in the nervous system. This anatamo-clinical ap-proach had early successes when the French anatomist and physi-cian Paul Broca visited the Bicêtre asylum in 1861 and examined a patient called Leborgne, who had progressively developed prob-lems in enunciating speech. After the death of Leborgne, Broca carried out an autopsy and identified an area of his brain that was damaged. He examined a second patient called Lelong, who had a very similar problem producing speech. After his death, Broca conducted an autopsy and found damage to the same area of the brain as Leborgne's. The anatamo-clinical approach flourished at the Bicêtre and then at the Salpêtrière Hospital where, as we shall learn in Chapter 3, Freud was taught the method by Jean-Martin Charcot.

THE TREATMENT OF NERVOUS DISEASES

Tuke and Pinel were advocates of treating the insane with dignity and respect. Their focus was on the care and treatment of the long-term inmates of asylums. For those who suffered from disorders that were less debilitating but still in need of remediation, the 18th and 19th centuries provided a whole range of 'cures'. These included rest cures, special diets, massage, hydrotherapy (treatment with jets of hot and cold water) and electrotherapy (local and general application of electric current). Of particular significance was the claim by Friedrich Anton Mesmer (1734–1815) that he had discovered a hitherto unknown fluid, which he called animal magnetism. This fluid, he said, could be manipulated and used to treat nervous ailments by inducing 'crises' in his patients, leading to a 'rebalancing' of their constitutions and bringing them back to health.

Mesmer became famous throughout Europe and his treatments were much sought after, although the medical establishment was highly critical of his increasing popularity with the public. In response to the concerns of the medical profession, the French government set up a royal commission to investigate Mesmer's claims. In 1784 the commission published a report which concluded that Mesmer had not discovered a magnetic fluid new to physics but which conceded that there was evidence that some patients had benefited from Mesmer's treatments. This the report attributed to the power of the imagination.

In the United Kingdom, James Braid (1795–1860) attended a demonstration of mesmerism by a visiting French mesmerist. He was impressed with the demonstration but was convinced that the effects of mesmerism could be understood without recourse to magnetism. Braid suspected that the altered state of consciousness produced by mesmerists was the result of the nerve centres of the brain becoming fatigued by, for example, staring at a bright light. He likened this state to a form of sleep which left the person open to suggestion and with decreased voluntary control of their actions. Braid called this state 'neurohypnotism', which eventually was shortened to 'hypnotism'. Freud was to use hypnotism as a form of treatment but, as we shall see in Chapter 3, he rejected it when he invented psychoanalysis.

A painting of a group undergoing mesmeric therapy in the late 18th century. The method acquired great popularity across Europe, though not all of the medical profession were convinced by Mesmer's claims.

James Braid, a Scottish surgeon and an amateur scientist, was one of the pioneers of hypnotherapy.

Key Points

- The publication of Johannes Müller's *Handbuch der Physiologie des Menschen für Vorlesungen* (*Handbook of Physiology*) provided a new understanding of the relationship between morphology and physiology for Freud's generation of medical researchers.

- Müller's concept of 'life energy' that left the body after death was rejected by his students as too closely resembling the religious concept of 'soul'.

- His students founded the *Deutsche Physikalische Gesellschaft* (German Physical Society) and vowed to explain physiological phenomena only in terms of physics and chemistry; one of them, Ernst Brücke, was to become Freud's mentor.

- Freud attended lectures by Franz Clemens Brentano, who proposed that psychology was to be the scientific study of mental phenomena and that the methodology for investigating mental phenomena was introspection.

- When Freud started his medical training in the 1870s, the treatment of mentally ill people was turning from mere containment in asylums to a more humane approach of compassion and the search for alleviation.

CHAPTER 2
Freud as zoologist, neurologist and physician

FREUD AS ZOOLOGIST, NEUROLOGIST AND PHYSICIAN

Freud came to fame as the inventor of psychoanalysis when he was in his early forties. As we shall see in Chapter 4, psychoanalysis was the result of a process of rigorous self-examination, conducted by a mature man who had already experienced a varied career, which had involved training and practising as a physician and carrying out research that included investigating the reproductive capacities of eels, uncovering the nervous system of crayfish and contributing to the methodology of anatomical investigation by inventing a staining technique to make cell bodies visible. He had also completed extensive studies of cerebral palsy, studied speech problems and become an advocate of the use of cocaine as an anaesthetic and stimulant.

Freud had an extensive set of publications behind him before psychoanalysis was born and could be considered to be a zoologist, neurologist and physician. In this chapter I shall explore these lesser known scientific contributions. As I shall discuss in later chapters, Freud believed that early experience and relationships had huge importance for later development. Many of the topics that he studied as a young man and the relationships he established with colleagues proved significant in his later theorizing, influencing the later development of psychoanalysis as both a scientific theory and an institution. A further justification for examining Freud's early career is because some of Freud's most trenchant critics have based their critiques on the honesty and integrity of Freud as a man. Knowing something of his background will help us to evaluate these critiques.

THE EARLY LIFE OF FREUD

In 1855, Jakob Freud (1815–96), a 41-year-old wool merchant residing in Freiberg, Moravia (now Příbor in the Czech Republic), married his (possibly) third wife, 21-year-old Amalia Nathanshon (1835–1930). Their son Schlomo Sigismund Freud was born one year later in 1856. The extended Freud family, comprising Jakob's adult sons Emanuel and Philip from his first marriage and

The eight-year-old Sigmund Freud with his father, Jakob.

Emanuel's children John and Pauline (respectively the same age and one year older than Sigismund), all lived in the same household. A year later, Jakob and Amalia had a second son, Julius, who died at the aged of six months when Sigismund was two years old.

The family moved to Leipzig and then on to Vienna when Sigismund was four years old and Jakob and Amalia were eventually to have eight children. The Freud family were non-practising Jews living in an antisemitic society and in later life Freud recalled his shame when his father did not retaliate after his hat was knocked off in an antisemitic incident. However, by

Freud's own account he had a happy childhood. His mother referred to him as 'my golden Sigi' and he asserted that 'A man who has been the indisputable favourite of his mother keeps for life the feeling of a conqueror, that confidence of success that often induces real success' (Freud, 1917, 1953). He was close to his nanny, Monika Zajic, and although she left the family when he was four, he dreamed about her more than 30 years later, when he was conducting his self-analysis.

The Freud children were well-educated and had middle-class aspirations for professional success, but the family were by no means rich. Freud had to seek bursaries to finance his studies and would always need to work to achieve an income. He was clearly a highly able and motivated schoolboy; he was enrolled at the Sperlgymnasium at the age of nine, a year younger than most of his classmates, and was soon top of his class, learning Greek, Latin, English and French among other subjects. Together with a school friend, Eduard Silberstein (1856–1925), he also taught himself Italian, as well as Spanish in order to read Cervantes in the original Spanish. Throughout his life, Freud drew on his strong background in the humanities and, as we shall see, used his knowledge of ancient Greek literature as a means of

Johann Wolfgang von Goethe, the leading German literary figure, was a great influence on the young Freud.

explaining his theories. When he was 17 Freud attended a lecture by the anatomist Carl-Bernhard Brühl (1820–1899), during which Brühl read an essay referencing Johann Wolfgang von Goethe (1749–1832) and his understanding of nature as a system of dynamic relationships that the scientist could decipher. This inspired Freud to study medicine rather than study law or enter the business world as his father had hoped.

FREUD THE MEDICAL STUDENT

In 1873, at the tender age of 17, Freud enrolled as a medical student at the University of Vienna. It was to take him eight years to qualify as a doctor at a time when most medical students graduated in five. It seems that Freud was simply in no rush to qualify and the medical curriculum at the University of Vienna allowed students a great deal of freedom to follow their interests. Freud took full advantage of this opportunity and took courses in philosophy with Franz Brentano, who distinguished between the mental and the material in terms of intentionality and was happy to accept the dualism of mind and matter. As we shall see, Freud also took the opportunity while at medical school to become involved in various research activities.

THE REPRODUCTIVE SYSTEM OF EELS

In 1876, Freud worked at the Institute of Comparative Anatomy, headed by Karl Claus (1835–99). There he took a course by Claus on general biology and Darwinism, which introduced him to a thorough-going naturalistic approach to understanding what it is to be human. At around this time, he began to question the value of philosophical thinking and embraced a fully empirical attitude to understanding the human condition. He ceased to attend philosophy lectures and described himself as being 'anti-philosophy' and distanced himself from Brentano.

While at the Institute of Comparative Anatomy, Freud was awarded a research scholarship to work at the Laboratory for Marine Zoology in Trieste, on Italy's Adriatic coast. At this research

Freud dissected hundreds of eels during his research into marine life as a young man.

station he was tasked to use his anatomical and microscopy skills to identify the male sexual organs of the eel. Over a period of weeks, Freud dissected more than 400 eels without success. The mystery of the absent organs was solved when Johannes Schmidt (1877–1933) found eel spawn in the Sargasso Sea in the North Atlantic Ocean, and arrived at the conclusion that the life cycle of the eel involves migration from European waters to the Sargasso Sea. It is only when eels are sexually active that testicles develop and this was the reason why the young Freud was unable to find them.

Freud did not particularly enjoy his time dissecting eels, but it gave him valuable research experience and demonstrated the complexity of sexual reproduction. He gained further zoological experience with Claus by dissecting other primitive fish, including the lamprey and the crayfish. Allied with his new-found interest in Darwinism, the importance of continuities and discontinuities of primitive and more advanced structures was becoming more and more salient.

FREUD IN THE LABORATORY

On his return to Vienna, Freud took a research post at the Physiological Institute at the University of Vienna. The Institute was run by Ernst Brücke, a physiologist who further instilled in Freud the value of systematic observation and the conviction that physiological phemomena must be understood in terms of underlying chemistry and physics. Freud considered his six years working with Brücke to be life-changing. At the Institute he met other like-minded scientists who were to become mentors and friends, including Josef Breuer (1842–1925) and Wilhelm Fliess (1858–1928). Breuer was older than Freud and a well-established medical doctor and physiologist; Fliess, two years older than Freud, was an ear, nose and throat specialist. These colleagues proved to be two of the most significant relationships at this stage of Freud's life. Both were instrumental in the development of psychoanalysis and provided Freud with sounding boards for his ideas as well as moral support when he was under attack from his critics.

However, neither of these friendships was to survive after psychoanalysis was established. Summing up his time with Brücke, Freud stated that at the Institute: 'I found rest and satisfaction – and men, too, whom I could respect and take as my models.' He also found some academic success, beginning his publishing career with scientific papers that included 'On the origin of the posterior nerve-roots in the spinal cord of the ammocoetes', 'Observations on the configuration and finer structure of the lobed organs in eels described as testes' and 'Note on a method for anatomical preparation of the nervous system.'

A portrait of the psychologist Joseph Breuer by the artist Emil Fuchs, 1897.

MILITARY SERVICE AND FREUD THE SMOKER

Freud was forced to take a break from his academic career in 1880, when he spent the year performing compulsory military service. For Freud this was a frustrating waste of time and one that was to have tragic consequences later in life, because it was during this period that he began smoking cigarettes and then the cigars which would become his trademark. Only three years later his friend Fliess advised him to stop smoking after he was diagnosed with heart problems brought on by excessive intake of nicotine from his 20 daily cigars. Freud stopped smoking for seven weeks but then started again, complaining that without smoking he could not function intellectually. In 1923 he was diagnosed with cancer of the palate and jaw and spent the rest of his life in constant pain, enduring 33 operations and wearing a series of specially designed protheses to keep his nasal cavity and mouth separate. He was well aware that mouth cancer would kill him but was so convinced of the importance of smoking cigars to his productivity that he refused to give them up a second time.

FREUD'S CAREER IN MEDICINE

After completing his military service, Freud returned to his studies and in 1881 finally graduated from medical school. He was still not keen to practise as a doctor; his interests remained focused on research. However, this path had to be modified when, in 1882, he met and fell in love with Martha Bernays (1861–1951).

Freud was now faced with the practical problem of how he could afford to marry and start a family. His solution was to commit to a medical career by developing a private practice as a neurologist while also keeping up his research by becoming an academic neuropathologist. With this goal in mind he gained experience of general medicine by working at the Vienna General Hospital under Hermann Nothnagel (1841–1905). In 1883, aged 27, he became an assistant to Theodor Hermann Meynert (1833–1892). Meynert was Professor of Neurology and Psychiatry at the University of Vienna and it was at Meynert's clinic in 1883 that

Freud, who had been most comfortable at the laboratory bench, gained his first significant experience of psychiatry and dealing with mentally ill patients.

A ground-breaking neuro–anatomist, Meynert had a string of anatomical firsts behind him and a list of eponymous brain structures including Meynert's bundle and Meynert's commissure. Assisting him suited Freud because Meynert's approach to psychiatry was grounded firmly in neurology. Meynert was committed to discovering the organic basis of psychiatric illness and in *The Diseases of the Forebrain*, published in 1884, he argued that insanity was the result of such diseases. For Meynert, psychological illness was unequivocally a result of underlying brain damage or lesions. He was to teach some of the most influential figures of 19th-century neurology, including Sergei Korsakoff (1854–1900), who studied alcoholic psychosis, and Karl Wernicke (1848–1905), who studied aphasia and is famous for identifying an area of the brain where damage through disease or injury produces highly specific problems in understanding written and

Sigmund Freud and his wife, Martha Bernays. The pair exchanged a romantic series of love letters before marrying.

spoken language. Wernicke and Meynert were proponents of so-called 'localization theory', which identified brain or nerve centres with highly specific functions. At the time, Freud the neurologist agreed with this theory, but in 1891, when he was publishing psychoanalytic works as well as works in neurology in his first full-length book, *On Aphasia*, Freud argued against the localization theory and developed a theory that focused on the relationships or dynamics between different brain or nerve centres as the key to understanding the relationship between brain and mind.

Karl Wernicke was a German neurologist who believed that mental illness was a result of defects in brain physiology.

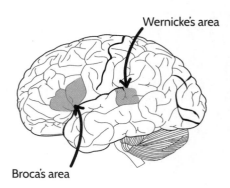

Karl Wernicke connected certain disorders with a particular region of the brain, which is now known as 'Wernicke's area'.

Wernicke's area

Broca's area

FREUD AND COCAINE

It was during Freud's four-year engagement to Martha that he became involved in one of the most controversial episodes of his career. Keen to step outside the shadows of Brücke and Meynert, Freud found a new medical rather than neurological problem to re-

research. This was an investigation into the effects and possible therapeutic value of the drug cocaine, which had been isolated from coca leaves in 1859. Freud became aware of its possibilities from a paper written by Theodor Aschenbrandt in 1883, which described the remarkable effects of the drug when administered to exhausted Bavarian soldiers. These effects included enhanced concentration, reduction of tiredness and suppression of hunger.

Theodor Meynert believed that mental illness derived from physical defects within the brain.

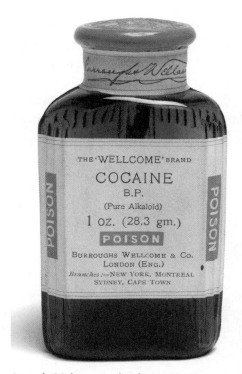

An early 20th-century bottle containing cocaine. Freud described cocaine as the 'wonder drug'.

Freud read the account with great interest and set about getting access to the drug. He experimented on himself and confirmed the results, publishing in 1884 a very positive account of the potential therapeutic benefits of cocaine in a pamphlet called 'Über *Coca*', believing that he might enhance his career by promoting a new 'wonder drug'.

Freud's enthusiasm for cocaine was such that he encouraged Martha to use it to treat a variety of minor ailments. Ever the careful observer, he noticed that there were marked individual differences in how his friends and colleagues responded to cocaine. He himself needed only small doses to reduce fatigue and aid concentration, but some of his colleagues and friends required increasingly large doses. It does not appear that at the time Freud saw this as a major concern. He also read with great interest research suggesting that the effects of cocaine were antagonistic to the effects of morphine, so cocaine might be used as a means of treating morphine addiction. His friend Ernst von Fleischl-Marxow (1846–91), who was an assistant to Brücke at the Physiological Institute, had become addicted to morphine after using it to dull the pain caused by an injury to his thumb so severe that amputation was required. On the advice of Freud, Fleischl-Marxow began using cocaine as a means of treating his morphine addiction, but sadly this resulted only in the formation of a new addiction; Fleischl-Marxow's health further deteriorated and he died tragically young at the age of 45.

Freud also recognized the pain-killing properties of the drug, but it was his colleague Kark Koller who made a name for himself in this respect, when he demonstrated the clinical value of cocaine as an anaesthetic during eye surgery.

ACADEMIC NEUROPATHOLOGY AND THE VISIT TO PARIS

In 1885, Freud became a *privatdozent* – a German academic title that qualified an academic to lecture without the supervision of a professor – and at this point his career appeared to be progressing in an orderly and not particularly surprising trajectory. He had made important contributions in a variety of fields and professionally he was securing his future by establishing himself in pri-

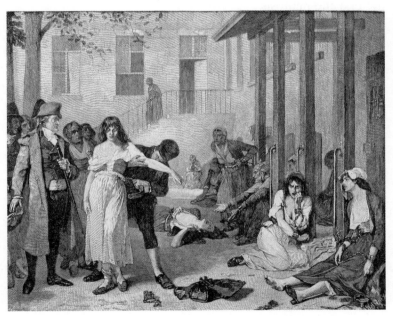

A painting by Tony Robert-Fleury shows the French psychologist Philippe Pinel treating patients at Salpêtrière Hospital in Paris.

vate practice as a neurologist and developing his academic career with his post at the University of Vienna. He had worked with some of the leading physiologists and neurologists of the day in a series of Viennese Institutes of international repute. His personal life was on track, and his marriage to Martha was planned for the next year. But as he approached the age of 30, his academic trajectory began to veer away from what appeared to be guaranteed Viennese professional respectability and take him in a direction that led to a brand new science, which he was to build on foundations considered contentious to this day. While it is unlikely that a single event was responsible for this change in direction, the award of a travelling scholarship to visit the Salpêtrière Hospital in Paris and study under Jean-Martin Charcot (1825–1893) was influential. In the next chapter we shall examine the importance of this visit and learn how Freud the microscopist and dissector of brains and eels became a practised hypnotist and therapist of hysteria and neurosis.

Key Points

- Freud grew up in a large and happy family, the favourite child of his mother.

- A highly able student, he gained a strong background in the humanities, which was to influence his theories.

- A conference on Goethe's argument that the world should be understood not as a giant machine manipulated by God or the souls of humans but as a structured whole that needed to be seen as a system of dynamic relationships influenced Freud's thinking at the age of 17.

- In 1873 Freud enrolled as a medical student at the University of Vienna, where he remained for eight years before graduating.

- In 1876, he studied Darwinism and rejected philosophical thinking.

- Mentoring from Ernst Brücke, Josef Breuer and Wilhelm Fliess contributed to the development of Freud's concept of psychoanalysis.

- As an assistant to Theodor Hermann Meynert (1833–1892), Professor of Neurology and Psychiatry at the University of Vienna, Freud gained his first experience with psychiatry and mentally ill patients.

CHAPTER 3
Freud the Neurologist

FREUD THE NEUROLOGIST

In 1882, Freud's friend and mentor Josef Breuer related to him the curious case of a 22-year old woman he had begun treating the previous year. This case had been particularly exhausting and troublesome, and Breuer estimated that he had spent around a thousand hours treating a baffling array of ever-changing symptoms. According to Breuer, his patient, who became known under the pseudonym 'Anna O', was bright and engaging and he judged her capable of great insight. Her problems had begun when her father succumbed to an illness that proved to be fatal. At this time Anna began to exhibit a wide variety of symptoms, including general weakness, paralysis, loss of appetite, exaggerated changes in mood, sleepwalking, amnesia, double vision and strange problems with language which resulted in her claiming that she could not speak her native German and could only respond to questions by speaking English. None of these symptoms could be linked to any obvious underlying physiological damage. The diagnosis made by Breuer was one of hysteria.

Breuer used the technique of free association to treat Bertha Pappenheim, who was identified in his case notes as 'Anna O.'

Breuer took Anna's symptoms seriously and it is clear that she had great trust in him, at one point refusing to take food from anyone else. He visited her for daily sessions and discovered that Anna would lapse into 'absences' where she seemed to take on another character and to be confused, often muttering to herself. Breuer began to repeat her words back to her and she elaborated on them, eventually getting into the habit of creating whole stories. Breuer observed that Anna's agitation was reduced after these sessions and Anna herself recognized that this simple activity helped to relieve her symptoms in a way that no other treatment had achieved; she began to talk about her 'talking cure' or 'chimney sweeping'. However, this relief was temporary, so Breuer began to look for a longer-term solution and started to build on the success of 'chimney sweeping' by hypnotizing Anna and asking her to remember when particular painful and unpleasant symptoms had first appeared and how she felt. Crucially, in her normal waking state, Anna had no memory of these occasions. Under hypnosis, as she described the events and her feelings, Anna's distress would increase but then entirely disappear. For example, her refusal to drink water disappeared after she remembered the occasion when an English companion drank from a glass of water that had been licked by the family's pet dog, eliciting in her feelings of disgust. Breuer told Freud that Anna was suffering from 'reminiscences' which had taken physical form – that is, the memory of the unpleasant event had been converted into a physical symptom and the recovery of the original memory allowed those unpleasant feelings to be experienced and let go. Breuer called this a process of 'catharsis' – the Greek word used to describe the emotional release that drama could produce in an audience.

FREUD AND NEUROPATHOLOGY

It was shortly after Breuer had treated Anna O that Freud was appointed *privatdozent* in Neuropathology at the University of Vienna. The role of *privatdozent* in the German university system is similar to that of visiting lecturer in the United Kingdom or adjunct or associate professor in the United States – the holder is qualified to lecture but does not have a permanent job at the university. This role gave Freud the opportunity to apply to the Academic Senate of the University of Vienna for a travelling bursary to visit the world-famous Salpêtrière Hospital in Paris to work with Jean-Martin Charcot and then to travel on to visit Berlin to study with the paediatrician Adolf Baginsky (1843– 1918). Freud's primary intention in applying for this travel bursary was to develop his understanding of neurology and to learn about the brain anatomy of children. Freud resolved to bring the case of Anna O to Charcot's attention and canvass his opinion on Breuer's innovative treatment. This trip, by Freud's own account, was to have a profound effect on his subsequent career, marking a shift from laboratory-based research to clinical practice. To understand why this trip was so important to Freud, it is necessary to understand a little about Jean-Martin Charcot and his research programme at the Salpêtrière.

NEW TREATMENTS AT THE SALPÊTRIÈRE HOSPITAL

In the 19th century, the classification, diagnosis and treatment of what we now characterize as psychiatric or neurological diseases was chaotic and contested. At the Salpêtrière Hospital in Paris, Jean-Martin Charcot (1825–93) was attempting to impose some order on this chaos. Charcot had taken over the role once filled by Philippe Pinel, and when Freud visited him in 1885 he was Super-intendent and Professor of Pathological Anatomy at the University of Paris. Under Charcot's direction the Salpêtrière, founded as an asylum for the destitute and unwanted of Paris, had become a model hospital that championed the dignified treatment of its patients and was a renowned centre for the scientific study of nervous disorders, employing the latest techniques such as microscopy and photography in order to research diagnosis and treatment.

Charcot's research programme was producing notable suc-cesses. He had made ground-breaking studies that led to the iden-

Jean-Martin Charcot was the superintendent of the Salpêtrière hospital when Freud visited in 1885.

tification of multiple sclerosis as a specific disease and its cause as damage to the myelin sheaths that surround nerves. Charcot was named as one of the discoverers of Charcot-Marie-Tooth disease (CMT), which is characterized by loss of sensation and muscle tissue in the limbs, and he had also identified amyotrophic lateral sclerosis (ALS) as a distinct motor neuron disease that results in weakened and wasted muscles. Charcot's success as a neurologist rested on his anatomo-clinical method which linked

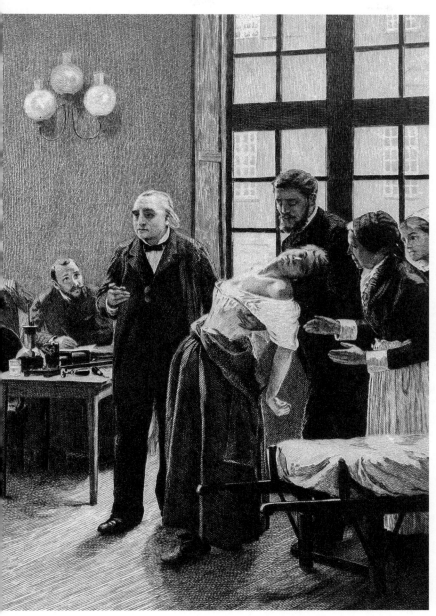

The painting Une leçon clinique à la Salpêtrière *by André Brouillet shows*
Charcot treating a patient for hysteria. A copy of this painting hung in Freud's
consulting room.

systematic observation and recording of symptoms over time with subsequent autopsy, in order to identify lesions in the brain and nervous system associated with those symptoms and those symptoms only. Charcot worked on the assumption that nervous diseases had physical causes and that these were inherited from one generation to another, representing a process of degeneration of the human race.

One of the most mysterious of the diseases that Charcot treated at the Salpêtrière was hysteria, which, of course, was the very illness diagnosed by Breuer in the case of Anna O. Charcot took a special interest in hysteria, challenging the then current understanding of the disease, which had been categorized since the time of the ancient Greeks as a female disorder – the name itself is derived from *hystera*, the Greek word for the uterus. In the second century CE, the Greek physician Galen had suggested that the symptoms of hysteria were the result of a lack of sexual activity which caused the uterus to travel around the body searching for gratification – the so-called 'wandering womb' theory. The treatment advice from physicians was to marry and have children. The theory that hysteria was a female disease had persisted into the 19th century, and both the incidence of hysteria and the range of symptoms that the medical establishment understood as hysterical – which included loss of sensation, paralysis, contractures (tensing of muscles) loss of voice and palpitations – were, if anything, increasing.

HYPNOTISM AND HYSTERIA

The patients who were resident at the Salpêtrière were nearly all women, many of whom had been diagnosed with hysteria. A small number of them – Marie 'Blanche' Wittmann (1859–1913), Augustine Gleizes (1861–unknown) and Geneviève Legrand (1843–unknown) – became famous because Charcot presented them to the public in regular Friday morning lectures to demonstrate the symptoms of hysteria. These lectures were attended not only by physicians and clinicians, but also by writ-

A photograph of Augustine Gleizes, who was diagnosed with hysteria, in her normal state upon admittance to the Salpêtrière hospital in 1878.

ers, actors, artists, journalists and the merely curious. However, despite making these women famous as hysterics, Charcot did not consider hysteria to be a female disease and was a key figure in breaking the link between the reproductive system and hysteria. He came to diagnose hysteria in male patients after treating men who had been involved in industrial accidents as outpatients and recognizing that their symptoms went beyond those that would be expected from the tissue damage resulting from the initial incident. He was also aware of the literature from the United States and the United Kingdom about so-called 'railway spine', a malady following injury resulting from train collisions, which demonstrated that a traumatic accident could produce emotional effects over and above those that would be expected by the physical injury. Over his career Charcot went on to diagnose more than 60 men with hysteria. He also diagnosed a number of children, which provided further support for his argument that hysteria was unconnected to the reproductive system since these children were not sexually mature.

While he had no hesitation in diagnosing cases of male hysteria, Charcot still held that there were important gender differences in how hysteria presented itself. He argued that male hysteria was primarily the result of trauma, giving the example of a man who had suffered a shoulder injury that had completely healed and whose hysterical symptoms of paralysis and numbness of the arm could be triggered by a light tap to the original site of the injury. According to Charcot, the tap on the shoulder was setting off the dynamic lesion that was, as it were, lying dormant in his nervous system. Charcot called this rekindling of the dynamic lesion akin to a spontaneous hypnotic state, 'autosuggestion'. This leads us to Charcot's account of hypnotism and its relation to hysteria.

In 1875 Charcot encountered a paper written by a medical student, Charles Richet (1850–1935), which suggested that hypnosis was the result of modifications to the underlying brain and nervous system and should be considered a form of neurosis.

Charles Richet, a French physiologist, won the Nobel Prize in Medicine in 1913 for his work on anaphylaxis.

Charcot accepted this argument and came to believe that hysteria and hypnosis were the results of a common cause, differing only in that hysteria was brought on by spontaneous auto-suggestion and hypnosis was the result of external suggestion by a hypnotist. Charcot experimented extensively with hypnotism,

Planche XXX.

HYSTÉRO-ÉPILEPSIE

A photograph showing the 'contracture' stage of hystero-epilepsy.

discovering that he could easily use the technique to hypnotize his patients who had been previously diagnosed with hysteria and induce full-blown hysterical episodes. Blanche, Augustine and Geneviève, identified to Charcot's Friday audience by their first names only, became famous, with Blanche becoming known as the 'Queen of the Hysterics'. At the instruction of Charcot, Désiré-Magloire Bourneville (1840–1909) and Paul-Marie-Léon Regnard (1850–1927) made photographic records of the phases of hysteria which were published in three volumes as the *Iconographie photographique de la Salpêtrière: service de M. Charcot.*

FREUD AT THE SALPÊTRIÈRE

Freud was so impressed by Charcot, both as a doctor and as a man, that he named his second child and first son Jean-Martin in his honour. Freud also kept a reproduction of the painting *A Clinical Lesson at the Salpêtrière* by Pierre Aristide Andre Brouillet (1857–1914) in his consulting rooms in Vienna; after he fled the Nazi regime in Austria in 1938 to set up home in London, he hung the print above the couch he used for psychoanalyzing his patients. To prolong his stay in Paris and to get to know Charcot better, Freud offered to translate a new collection of Charcot's lectures into German.

When Freud eventually had the opportunity to raise the case of Anna O to Charcot, the great man expressed little interest. Freud himself put the case of Anna O out of his mind and after visiting Baginsky in Berlin he returned to Vienna and started in private practice as a neurologist. He wrote an account of his time in Paris and Berlin and a short paper on Charcot, then began to make a living from patients who came to him looking for help with their various nervous disorders. At this time Freud treated his patients with the array of therapeutic methods used by his contemporaries, including electrotherapy (the application of electric shocks targeting either a specific area or the whole of the body), cold and hot baths and, increasingly, hypnotism. Freud

Hippolyte Bernheim was a member of the Nancy School of Hynposis and put forward the theory of suggestibility.

had learned from Charcot how to induce hysterical symptoms using hypnotism, but the latter had not been interested in it as a therapeutic method. Its therapeutic use had been developed by the Nancy School of Hypnosis, led by Ambroise-Auguste Liébeault (1823–1904) and Hippolyte Bernheim (1840–1919). The members of the Nancy school took a diametrically opposite approach to Charcot on hypnotism. They believed that hypnotism and hysteria were not the result of hereditary brain degeneration, arguing instead that all of us are susceptible to the influence of others and that hypnotic states are akin to sleep – occasions when we are not fully conscious and therefore more open to influence. Between 1888 and 1892 Freud began to study the therapeutic use of hypnotism intensively and in the summer of 1889 he travelled to France to study with Bernheim.

RETURN TO THE CATHARTIC METHOD

It was also in 1889 that Freud started treating a patient referred to as 'Emmy von N'. Emmy suffered depression, aches and pains, tics and involuntary movements. To begin with Freud advised the usual treatments of massage, rest and baths, but during daily vis-its to her in a sanatorium, he discovered that she could easily be hypnotized. He then attempted to use suggestion to remove her various symptoms. However, what he discovered was that under hypnosis the conversations with Emmy turned again and again to her memories. Remembering Breuer's cathartic method, Freud began to systematically explore them and instead of suggesting that the symptoms should simply go away he encouraged Emmy to examine her memories and the feelings they evoked. As Breuer had found in the case of Anna O six years previously, this resulted in the symptoms disappearing. For the next three years, Freud used hypnosis and the cathartic method to treat his hysterical patients.

This was to change in 1892, when Freud was asked to treat a young woman who was suffering from pains in her legs which were making it difficult for her to walk. He initially treated her

A photograph of Sigmund Freud in 1891.

legs with small electric shocks, which proved ineffective. Fräulein Elisabeth von R, as he called her, was the youngest daughter from a wealthy family. She stated that she didn't want to get married and was content to stay at home and look after her father, whom she loved very much. He was ill with heart disease, and she looked after him until he died. After his death her elder sisters married and, sadly, her second sister died from heart failure too. At this time Elisabeth began to complain of leg pains and problems walking. When Freud began the cathartic treatment, the first problem he faced was that Elisabeth would not be hypnotized. Breuer was convinced that hypnosis was necessary because memories that had been forgotten could only be accessed in a hypnoid state. With hypnosis not available as a therapeutic method, Freud simply asked Elisabeth to lie down on a couch. He placed his hand on her forehead and instructed her to tell him everything that went through her mind when he pressed hard on her head. At the signal of the application of pressure on her forehead and through careful questioning Elisabeth eventually revealed that the pains in her leg were at the spot where her father used to rest his leg on hers while she changed his bandages. Freud carried on with the treatment and was able to slowly remove her symptoms one by one as she revealed more and more about herself.

During one session, Elisabeth's widowed brother-in-law could be heard outside Freud's office. At the sound of his voice Elisabeth's leg pains returned with great intensity, from which Freud inferred that she was in love with her brother-in-law and that this was at the root of her hysterical symptoms. Going beyond the bounds of what today we would think acceptable in a doctor-patient relationship, Freud spoke to Elisabeth's mother and asked if her daughter could marry her brother-in-law. He was told that such a match was inappropriate and the matter was dropped. Some time later Freud saw Elisabeth at a party and concluded that his treatment had cured her of hysteria since she was dancing beautifully with no sign of problems with her legs. For Freud, this was a significant case because he had cured a patient without the use of hypnosis, instead asking her to say the first things that came into her consciousness.

STUDIES IN HYSTERIA

Freud now began to use the cathartic method almost exclusively, with or without the use of hypnotism. His relationship with Breuer was becoming increasingly strained for he was beginning to reject Breur's understanding of hysteria as a separate hypnoid state split off from other mental processes, instead seeing it as continuous with the rest of psychic life. Breuer was also resistant to Freud's growing interest in the sexual basis of hysteria. It was in this context of increasing personal tension and theoretical disagreements that they worked on a joint publication, which was to become *Studies in Hysteria*, published in 1895. In it, Breuer finally gave a full account of the treatment of Anna O and made explicit his cathartic method. Freud described the cases of Elisabeth von R and Emmy von N. The symptoms of hysteria were to be understood as the result of traumatic memories that had been repressed to save the patient from distress. Nevertheless, the excitation caused by these memories was still active and had been converted into physical symptoms that symbolized the memory of the traumatizing event. The cathartic method allowed the patient to go back to the event and to deal with the feelings and emotions associated with it there and then, eliminating the need for the production of symptoms – a process known as abreaction.

THE SEXUAL NATURE OF NEUROSES

By the time *Studies in Hysteria* was published, Freud's relationship with Breuer was broken. Freud now fully embraced the importance of sexuality in human development in general and in the development of hysteria. The final empirical evidence to back up his theory came from a review of the patients he had personally treated for hysteria using the cathartic method. He noted that in all the cases, including one of hysteria combined with obsessional thoughts, the patients reported early sexual experiences of which

A bust of the Austro-German psychiatrist Richard von Krafft-Ebing.

they were not aware before analysis. Of these patients, twelve were women and eight were men. Freud wrote to Wilhelm Fliess that no neurosis or case of neurasthenia existed without evidence of some kind of sexual disturbance.

THE SEDUCTION THEORY

Freud wrote about the seduction theory and the observations it was based upon in a series of three papers published in 1896: *Heredity and the Aetiology of the Neuroses, Further Remarks on the Neuro-Psychoses of Defence* and *The Aetiology of Hysteria*. In these publications Freud proposed, rather euphemistically, a 'seduction theory' of hysteria, which was in effect a theory that identified child sexual abuse as its cause.

According to the seduction theory, the road to hysteria and neurosis begins when the child is the victim of a sexual assault. Since the child is not sexually mature the traumatic sexual assault makes no sense and cannot be understood, so the memory is repressed and held as an unconscious memory. If the memory is brought to consciousness after puberty and understood, no hysterical or neurotic symptoms develop, but if the memory is too painful to deal with it is kept out of consciousness through the process of defence and repression. Once these defences begin to break down and the repressed memory begins to return, it is converted into somatic symptoms in an attempt to stop memory and feelings returning.

Freud presented the seduction theory to the Society of Psychiatry and Neurology at the University of Vienna, where the reception was unenthusiastic. Richard Krafft-Ebing (1840–1902) who was renowned for cataloguing sexual behaviour, remarked: 'It sounds like a scientific fairy tale.' Within 18 months, Freud was to give up his seduction theory of hysteria and develop the technique and theory of psychoanalysis.

Key Points

- Josef Breuer discovered the cathartic method when treating a young hysterical woman named 'Anna O' in 1883.

- In 1885, Freud visited the neurologist Jean-Martin Charcot at the Salpêtrière Hospital in Paris and learned about hysteria and hypnotism.

- In 1889, Freud visited Nancy in France to learn about hypnotic suggestion.

- In 1892, Freud treated Fräulein Elisabeth von R with Breuer's cathartic method.

- Freud and Breuer published *Studies in Hysteria* (1895), in which hysteria was understood as the defence against the return of traumatic memories.

- In 1895, Freud tried to tie his clinical work to the underlying structure and organization of the nervous system.

- In 1898, Freud's association with Breuer ended after Freud presented the seduction theory of neuroses.

CHAPTER 4

The birth of psychoanalysis

THE BIRTH OF PSYCHOANALYSIS

From the mid-1890s to the start of the new century, Freud's understanding of neurology, psychology and the treatment of hysteria and neuroses changed dramatically. It is during this period that he invented psychoanalysis as a novel method for investigating mental processes, treating nervous disorders and understanding psychology as more than the study of conscious experience. Though he modified, elaborated and extended his ideas until his death in 1939, it was in this period that the basic psychoanalytic conceptual scheme was laid down.

In 1895, the year of the publication of *Studies in Hysteria*, Freud identified dreams as the disguised fulfilment of prohibited wishes. This deceptively simple observation was to provide the starting point for Freud's account of the structure and function of the mind and by 1900, when *The Interpretation of Dreams* was published, he was ready to announce the birth of a new scientific approach to psychology.

DREAMS AND FREE ASSOCIATION

After failing to hypnotize Elisabeth von R, Freud had resorted to asking her to report on everything that came into her head when he pressed his hand on her forehead and asked her questions (see p.63). By using this method, he was able to work with her responses to reveal content that had previously been hidden and was thus able to rid her of her hysterical symptoms. The simple order to honestly report the first things that come into one's consciousness is the basic principle of the method of free association which Freud began using to explore his own mental life, starting with the content of his dreams.

THE INTERPRETATION OF DREAMS

In *The Interpretation of Dreams*, Freud provides both interpretations of his own dreams and accounts of dreams collected from his family and friends. In total, he mentions about 50 of his dreams and their links to more than 40 of his childhood memories. The

Sigmund Freud published The Interpretation of Dreams *in 1900. Eight editions of the book were printed in Freud's lifetime.*

dream that resulted in his new understanding of the mind occurred on the night of 23–24 July. This dream, which he wrote
up as 'The Dream of Irma's Injection' he presented as a 'specimen'
dream which could be used by his readers to understand how
he carried out his analysis and thus provide a starting point for
them to interpret their own dreams. As well as demonstrating
the process of dream analysis, Freud explained the processes by
which dreams were created – the so-called 'dream-work' – and
the fundamental reason that leads to the creation of dreams in the
first place. Freud's account of the circumstances that prompted
the dream and his account of the dream itself are given below.

THE DREAM OF IRMA'S INJECTION
One day I had a visit from a junior colleague, who had been
staying with my patient, Irma, and her family at their coun-
try resort. I asked him how he had found her, and he an-
swered, 'She's better, but not quite well.' I was conscious that
my friend Otto's words, or the tone in which he spoke them,
annoyed me. I fancied I detected a reproof in them, such
as to the effect that I had promised the patient too much
. . . That same evening, I wrote out Irma's case history, with
the idea of giving it to Dr M, a common friend, in order to
justify myself. That night I had the following dream, which I
noted down immediately upon waking.

Dream of July 23rd–24th, 1895
A large hall – numerous guests, whom we were receiving.
– Among them was Irma. I at once took her to one side,
as though to answer her letter and to reproach her for not
having accepted my 'solution' yet. I said to her: 'If you still
get pains, it's really only your fault.' She replied: 'If you only
knew what pains I've got now in my throat and stomach and

abdomen – it's choking me.' – I was alarmed and looked at her. She looked pale and puffy. I thought to myself that after all I must be missing some organic trouble. I took her to the window and looked down her throat, and she showed signs of recalcitrance, like women with artificial dentures. I thought to myself that there was really no need for her to do that. She then opened her mouth properly and on the right I found a big white patch; at another place I saw extensive whitish-grey scabs upon some remarkable curly structures which were evidently modelled on the turbinal bones of the nose. – I at once called in Dr M, and he repeated the examination and confirmed it. . . . Dr M looked quite different from usual; he was very pale, he walked with a limp and his chin was clean-shaven. . . . My friend Otto was now standing beside her as well, and my friend Leopold was percussing her through her bodice and saying: 'She has a dull area low down on the left.' He also indicated that a portion of the skin on her left shoulder was infiltrated. (I noticed this, just as he did, in spite of her dress.) . . . M said: 'There's no doubt it's an infection, but no matter; dysentery will supervene and the toxin will be eliminated.' . . . We were directly aware, too, of the origin of the infection. Not long before, when she was feeling unwell, my friend Otto had given her an injection of a preparation of propyl, propyls . . . propionic acid . . . trimethylamin (and I saw before me the formula for this printed in heavy type) . . . Injections of this sort ought not to be given so thoughtlessly . . . And probably the syringe had not been clean. (Freud 1900)

To understand the dream, Freud takes as his starting point that the dream has meaning and is not a random jumble of images produced, perhaps, by the spontaneous firings of nerve cells. However, the content and events in the dream are very odd and in the cold light of day are not coherent or logical. It is here that the method of free association comes into play. Freud takes each element in the dream and writes down the spontaneous thoughts that these elements evoke. Through this process of free association Freud concluded that in the dream Otto was punished for his implied criticism of Freud's treatment and Freud's reputation as a competent and professional doctor was restored. Freud reported that he had gone to bed worried and angry, wishing ill on his friend, and in his dream this wish for revenge on Otto had been fulfilled. Freud was so convinced of the analysis of this dream that in a letter to Fliess, he wrote 'Do you think that one day there will be a marble tablet on the house, saying: "In this house on July 24, 1895, the Secret of Dreams was revealed to Dr Sigmund Freud?"'

A DREAM IS THE FULFILMENT OF A WISH

The crucial observation for Freud was that the dream was a fulfilment of a wish and that this was the case with all dreams – a wish being a desire that was likely to be denied or prohibited rather than a simple want. If we want something we will try to get it, while a wish implies that there is something that is holding us back from directly trying. Freud gave the example of his daughter Anna's dream after she had been sent to bed without dinner because she had been sick earlier in the day – the result, according to her nurse, of having eaten too many strawberries. In the night Anna was heard shouting in her sleep: 'Anna Freud strawberries, wild strawberries, omelette and pudding.' In real life she had been not been allowed dinner nor her favourite strawberries, but in the dream she had eaten both garden strawberries and wild strawberries – a double portion of strawberries. What she had been denied in real life she had satisfied in a dream.

A child's wish for strawberries is harmless, but some of our wishes may be deeply troublesome. For example, saying out loud that one has wished for the death of a parent or sibling or to have sex with a relative is likely to result to shock and upset those who hear these sentiments expressed because there are strong social prohibitions

A photograph of Anna Freud in 1912.

against killing one's family or committing incest. These wishes can be too powerful to admit even to oneself. According to Freud, such wishes cannot be simply removed, but they can be censored so they do not reach consciousness. The dream is the product of a process of dream-work which disguises the underlying wish so that it can be expressed without fully revealing its unacceptable content.

DREAM-WORK

When Freud examined his associations to the elements in the dream, he found that they took him to places very different from where he started. He introduced the terms 'manifest content' and 'latent content' to distinguish between what the dream seems to be about and what it is really about.

The starting point of dream-work is what Freud called 'day residues', which comprise the wishes that have not been fulfilled during the day, and the unfulfilled wishes that were activated in early childhood. One reason why dreams are so complicated to understand is that, according to Freud, multiple wishes may be present in the same dream, requiring careful teasing apart. He identified four different aspects of dream-work.

Condensation

The happenings in dreams sometimes appear straightforward, but more usually dreams are jumbled and strange. Freud points out that most dreams are not constrained by the laws of physics, logic or narrative structure. People and places from different times might all appear in the same dream and there may be jumps from one scene to another which are impossible in real life. In the dream of Irma's Injection, the process of free association revealed to Freud that Dr M was both his friend Breuer and his older brother. Free association revealed that Irma in the dream also represented one of Irma's friends and a third woman who was one of Freud's friends. It is a characteristic of dreams that they may be very short, but analysis reveals that they are the result of putting together complex and convoluted chains of events and people. A huge amount of material may be condensed into a very short dream sequence.

Displacement

In the dream, Freud chides Otto for thoughtlessly giving Irma an injection and not even bothering to use a clean needle. Free association leads Freud to realize that he was actually chiding himself for the poor treatment of Irma but had shifted this unacceptable thought onto Otto. This is an example of displacement – shifting feelings, characteristics and identities onto other people or objects.

Representation

In dream-work, complex narratives are turned into images. Freud rejects the idea that it is possible to write a dream dictionary which indicates what each image symbolizes, though he does suggest that some images regularly represent particular objects – for example, a purse or box often symbolizes the vagina and a cigar a penis. However, this cannot be taken for granted and the meaning of an image needs to be worked out through free association and not simply assumed by the analyst.

Secondary revision

The processes of condensation, displacement and representation collect together a diverse set of events, people, symbols and feelings. Secondary revision is the attempt to fit this into some format that has the semblance of coherence. If the dream were too incoherent and nonsensical, it would disturb the dreamer, who would wake up. The secondary revision is the part of the dream-work which comes at the end of the process.

FREUD'S SELF-ANALYSIS

The discovery that dreams are the disguised fulfilment of wishes was the first stage of the creation of psychoanalysis. The second stage was Freud's self-analysis, which took place two years later. Freud announced the start of it in a letter to Fliess on 14 August 1897, telling his friend that he had become his own 'chief patient'. He went on to say that this self-analysis was the most difficult clinical work that he had ever attempted. The immediate trigger for it was the death of his father in 1896 and his concerns about his professional practice, which was struggling because he was attracting few new patients and the progress of those he was treating was frustratingly slow. Experiencing feelings of self-doubt and professional insecurity, Freud set about systematically learning about himself by analyzing his own dreams, hoping to understand his own anxieties. During this period Freud's friendship with Fliess became increasingly significant, and before examining the results of Freud's self-analysis it is useful to learn more about Fliess.

THE IMPORTANCE OF FLIESS

Freud met Wilhelm Fliess in 1887 through an introduction by Breuer, who had recommended that Fliess should attend Freud's lectures at the University of Vienna. Two years younger than Freud, Fliess soon displaced Breuer as his closest confidante. By training he was an otorhinolaryngologist – a specialist in conditions related to the ear, nose and throat. The correspondence between Freud and Fliess began straight away and continued until 1904, when their friendship broke down over an argument about who had first suggested that bisexuality was developmentally the primary sexual orientation. During their 17-year friendship, Freud placed great trust in Fliess and they both shared their theoretical speculations as well as personal confidences. Freud wrote more than 200 letters to Fliess, which revealed much about his creation of psychoanalysis. These were published in the 1950s, but as Freud burnt all of the letters that Fliess sent to him, our knowledge of their correspondence is one-sided.

Fliess too was interested in neuroses and problems in general psychology, physiology and biology, in particular the role of the nose and nasal cavity in human sexuality. Indeed, in the dream of Irma's Injection, it is noteworthy that when Freud examined Irma's throat he found turbinal bones, which are the bones that curl down into the nasal cavity and are covered in mucus over which air passes when we breathe in; this was clearly a reference to Fliess. In a controversial theory, Fliess proposed that there was a connection between the nose and the sexual system. This was based on the observation that women have increased frequency of nosebleeds during menstruation and that the nose is the only part of the body other than the genitals that is made up of erectile tissue (in the nose, this swells to reduce or increase the flow of air into the nasal cavity when the weather is hot, cold, wet or dry). In 1893 Fliess published *The Nasal Reflex Neurosis*, presenting his theory to the scientific community.

Freud's trust and confidence in Fliess was so great that he allowed him to operate on his nasal cavity and encouraged one of his patients, Emma Eckstein (1865–1924), to agree to the same operation. This went horribly wrong and Eckstein suffered from continuous nose bleeds. During corrective surgery it was discovered that Fliess had negligently left a long strip of gauze in the nasal cavity. Despite this terrible mistake, Freud continued the friendship and allowed Fliess to conduct two further operations on his own nose. The importance of Fliess at this time is that Freud kept Fliess up to date with the progress of his self-analysis and at the same time extensively discussed the importance of sexuality in human development.

A photograph of Sigmund Freud and Wilhelm Fliess in 1890. The two were introduced by Joseph Breuer and worked closely for many years.

Emma Eckstein was one of Freud's patients. Later, she became a psychoanalyst too.

INFANTILE SEXUALITY

One of the first results of Freud's self-analysis was the repudiation of his seduction theory. In a letter to Fliess in 1897, only 18 months after he had presented the theory to his peers, he wrote, 'I no longer believe in my neurotica.' In this sentence he turned his back on the theory that hysteria was the result of repressed memories of trauma (Breuer's theory) and of repressed memories of sexual trauma (the seduction theory). One of the reasons he set down for his abandonment of the theory which he had expected to lead to great interest and personal acclaim was that he was compelled to acknowledge that the cathartic method rarely, if ever, led to a completed analysis. Instead, symptoms removed by the process of abreaction were replaced by other symptoms and it was necessary to carry on with the treatment.

A second reason was that despite acknowledging the existence of widespread child sex abuse, Freud recognized that when he was treating hysterical or obsessional symptoms in a clinical setting, it was always the father who was identified as the abuser. This led Freud to believe that there was something special about father/child relationship in these reports of abuse. Further reasons for giving up the seduction theory were that after his forays into developing an account of psychology for neurologists and the distinction that he made in that work between primary and secondary processes he could not say, on the basis of a clinical analysis, whether his patients were reporting real events or fantasies; and patients who suffered from psychosis, a condition in which repression no longer functioned effectively, did not mention sexual abuse by their fathers in the fragments of discourse that they produced. However, Freud made it clear in his letter to Fliess that giving up the seduction theory did not leave him feeling depressed or disappointed, contrary to his expectations; instead he felt triumphant, because the building blocks of psychoanalysis were now in place.

PSYCHOANALYSIS AND THE FIRST TOPOGRAPHY

It is now possible to pull together the results of the dream analysis and Freud's self-analysis. Through the analysis of dreams Freud had recognized that dreams were the fulfilments of wishes. Some of our wishes are so dangerous that they are not allowed to become conscious (Cs) because the sexual content of those wishes is prohibited. At this time Freud first starts to mention the importance of the play *Oedipus Rex*, which deals with the tragic consequences of King Oedipus killing his father and committing incest with his mother (see p.145).

Our prohibited wishes do not simply dissipate over time or spontaneously disappear; they remain active in the unconscious (Ucs) and seek fulfilment. We get a glimpse of these wishes through our dreams but, even in a dream, these wishes are prevented from

A scene from Sophocles' play Oedipus Rex.

A photograph of Sigmund Freud at his desk in 1930.

becoming fully conscious through the process of dream-work – they are disguised. In our everyday life these prohibited wishes are kept unconscious through processes of defence and repression, which work to censor inappropriate material from reaching the conscious mind. Material of which we are not currently conscious but which is not subject to defence and repression and can be acccessed at will is designated as Preconscious (Pcs). This basic model – which conceptualized the conscious, unconscious and preconscious as separate but connected systems subject to censorship – became known as Freud's first topography and was first presented in the seventh chapter of *The Interpretation of Dreams*. As we shall see in Chapter 6, this model was replaced in the 1920s by a second topography that introduced the triad of id, ego and superego.

The year after *The Interpretation of Dreams* appeared, Freud published *The Psychopathology of Everyday Life* (1901). In this book he catalogued the ways in which disguised wishes could be discovered in our normal waking life in the parapraxes (slips of the tongue), simple mistakes and lapses of memory that we make on a daily basis. By moving his analysis outside the clinic, Freud showed that psychoanalysis is relevant not just to the study of neuroses and hysteria but to anyone who wishes to understand our normal human functioning.

Freud went on to elaborate his conceptual scheme by working with more patients suffering from different kinds of nervous disorders and to teach psychoanalysis to others. In the next chapter we shall turn to Freud's most important case histories. These illustrate how Freud developed his theory through dream analysis and give a clearer idea of what it was like to be psychoanalyzed by Sigmund Freud himself.

Key Points

- In 1895, Freud embraced dream analysis and recognized dreams as the fulfilment of wishes.

- In 1897, he began his own self-analysis.

- In 1897, he repudiated his seduction theory in letters to Fliess. The following year, he began to write a book about dreams.

- *The Interpretation of Dreams* was published in 1900, explaining the process of dream-work.

- Freud had shifted from a position of understanding neuroses as a problem of reminiscence to one of dealing with impulses and instincts.

CHAPTER 5
The case histories

Freud used case studies to justify, explain and illustrate his psycho-analytic research and writings, and these played the same role as the collection and analysis of quantitative data drawn from experiment, surveys or observational studies in other sciences. These case studies are, therefore, of fundamental importance for psychoanalysis.

Out of the 120 or so patients that Freud treated, only four of them were written up as extended case studies; a fifth case study was based not on his direct clinical experience of treating a client but on the autobiography of a patient who had been incarcerated in a psychiatric hospital and had never had any contact with Freud. These case studies were all published between 1905 and 1918. After 1918, for the rest of his career as an analyst, Freud mentioned other patients but did not write them up as extended studies.

The extended case studies have been put under much critical scrutiny ever since they were first published. Used by generations of psychoanalysts to understand Freud's clinical practice, they have become renowned in their own right as classics of the psycho_analytic literature. The patients, 'Dora', 'Rat Man', 'Little Hans', 'Wolf Man' and Daniel Schreber, have become famous too. After Freud's death, much effort was made to discover the true identities of these patients in order to learn more about their biographies, check the veracity of his accounts and assess the long-term efficacy of his treatment.

THE USE OF THE CASE STUDY

Freud was conscious that in the practice of psychoanalysis, the skills of dissection and microscopic observation employed in earlier years were replaced by the dialogue he held with his patients as they searched for the unconscious wishes that had brought them to his consulting rooms. He was somewhat uncomfortable about writing up case studies rather than presenting directly observable evidence and was concerned that they may lack the serious stamp of science. Nevertheless, the case studies became some of his most powerful tools to explain psychoanalysis and convince others of its importance.

To gain some understanding of psychoanalysis, it is useful to read Freud's case studies. This is not an easy undertaking, as Freud attempts to reflect the complexities of the clinical situation and often mixes description and analysis. He interprets dreams using the method of free association to identify unconscious infantile wishes, but the nature of resistance and repression and the processes of displacement and condensation mean that the reader who was not present at the analysis has to trust Freud that the sometimes dizzying interpretations make sense.

DORA: AN ANALYSIS OF A CASE OF HYSTERIA

The first of Freud's extended case studies presents the case of 'Dora'. This study ends on a note of therapeutic failure because Dora decided to terminate her own treatment, much to Freud's surprise. According to Freud, the value of this case study, even though it was left unfinished, was that it provided an explicit example of the clinical value of dream analysis that he had only recently introduced in *The Interpretation of Dreams* and also demonstrated the roots of complex hysterical symptoms in sexual impulses. Dora's treatment was relatively brief, lasting only three months in 1900, yet it took five years for Freud to write up the case and publish it in 1905 as *Fragment of an Analysis of a Case of Hysteria*. It is clear that he brooded over the case of Dora and it was through this he came to have a deeper understanding of the concept of transference (see p.98).

Freud begins the case study by telling us about the history of Dora's symptoms and her family background. Aged 18, Dora suffered from a variety of symptoms including loss of voice (aphonia), depression, problems breathing and the sensation that her throat was constricted and she would choke. She was also prone to fainting and had threatened suicide. This meant that she exhibited the classic symptoms of hysteria, which most neurologists of the time would have treated using hypnotic suggestion or

A letter by Sigmund Freud to Wilhelm Fliess explaining the Dora case.

electrotherapy; in cases of aphonia a common treatment was to administer electric current to the throat in an attempt to physically affect damaged or malfunctioning nerves. With the firm belief that repressed sexual wishes were the source of hysterical symptoms, Freud began his treatment using his new method of psychoanalysis.

Freud was acquainted with Dora's family – her parents and an older brother – but it soon became apparent that he was not aware of the full complexity of their interrelationships. The parents were good friends with a family referred to as the Ks and it

Ida Bauer, with her brother Otto, was given the pseudonym 'Dora' by Freud. She was the subject of one of his most important case studies.

Symptoms of hysteria began to appear for Dora after a holiday to their lakeside home. Freud believed that her memory of a kiss by the lake had taken the place of a repressed memory.

seemed to be an open secret that Dora's father was having a sexual relationship with Frau K. Dora knew about this affair and had become convinced that her father was offering her to Herr K as the price for his continued relationship with Frau K. Dora loved her father but also deeply resented that he would consider such an exchange and cared nothing for her feelings about it.

Dora's symptoms began to appear after a holiday with the K family at their lakeside home. During this holiday, she told her father that Herr K had made sexual advances towards her which she had rejected. Herr K was challenged by her father and strenuously denied that he had done anything improper; he told her father that Dora was reading inappropriate books and was merely fantasizing. Dora's father took the side of Herr K, believing him rather than his daughter. Back in Vienna, as Dora's symptoms became more severe, her father took her to see Freud.

Freud begins his analysis by disbelieving Dora's testimony of a lakeside kiss, as had her father. He describes it as a 'screen memory', a term he employed to refer to memories of usually innocuous events which displaced memories of repressed sexual experiences. In this case Freud argued that the supposed kiss at the lake was actually referring to an earlier incident which had occurred when Dora was 13 and had so upset her it had been repressed. At that time Herr K had invited Dora to his office to watch a parade. After carefully arranging that they would be alone together Herr K took hold of Dora and kissed her on the lips. Dora said she was disgusted and pushed him away. Freud interpreted this disgust not as the report of a sexual assault but as a hysterical symptom, arguing that a healthy 13-year-old girl must have been aroused by this sexual contact. He inferred that Dora had felt Herr K's erect penis against her body and her later symptoms of choking and loss of voice were displacements of unacceptable feelings of arousal and sexual desire. Bluntly, the choking and loss of voice were the result of Dora repressing her desires for oral sex with Herr K.

According to Freud, Dora had unacceptable sexual impulses towards both her father and Herr K. The sexual basis of her symp-

According to Freud, the jewellery box in Dora's dream symbolized her virginity.

toms was illustrated in the interpretation of two dreams. Freud noted down Dora's account of the first dream:

'A house was on fire. My father was standing beside my bed and woke me up. I dressed quickly. Mother wanted to stop and save her jewel-case; but Father said: "I refuse to let myself and my two children be burnt for the sake of your jewel-case." We hurried downstairs, and as soon as I was outside I woke up.'

Using the method of free association, Freud asked Dora to give her spontaneous reactions to the dream content. According to Freud's interpretation of the string of associations, the jewel case symbolized Dora's virginity which was under threat from Herr K and she wished to escape from Herr K with her father. In the second dream, which was much longer, Dora recounted walking around in a strange town. She found the house where she was living and there she discovered a letter from her mother, informing her that her father was dead and calling her back home.

She headed at once towards the station, passing through a thick wood and feeling unable to get any nearer to her destination. On meeting an unknown man who offered to take her to the station, she refused his help. She suddenly found herself at home and the servant told her that her mother and brother were at the cemetery. According to Freud, the man in the wood symbolized Herr K and the thick forest and town square that Dora walked through symbolized her sexual organs.

By analyzing these dreams and helping Dora to understand that her symptoms were the result of her repressed desires, Freud was convinced that he was making therapeutic progress. He was surprised when she turned up at his consulting rooms and told him that she was not having any further treatment. After some reflection, Freud concluded that during the analysis Dora had been treating him at various times as her father and as Herr K and was acting out her relations with them rather than with Sigmund Freud her doctor. Freud called this effect 'transference'. At first he thought of it as an obstacle to treatment, but then he began to develop the tendency to see the therapist in terms of previous relationships as an essential part of treatment instead. He went on to consider the phenomenon of countertransference, when the analyst reads back into the patient his or her own resistances and defences (see p.130).

RAT MAN: A CASE OF OBSESSIONAL NEUROSIS

This is one of the few cases that Freud himself considered a complete success. In it, he demonstrated that psychoanalysis could be used to treat not only hysteria but also obsessions. 'Rat Man' was later identified as Ernst Lanzer (1878–1919). Freud treated Lanzer for several months in 1907–08 and published the case history in 1909 in the newly founded *Jahrbuch für psychoanalytische und psychopathologische Forschungen* (Annals of Psychoanalytic and Psychopathological Research).

In 'Notes upon a Case of Obsessional Neurosis', Freud described the three-month treatment of the 29-year-old Lanzer.

Sigmund Freud's 'Notes Upon a Case of Obsessional Neurosis' from 1909. The subject in question was described in the case notes as the 'Rat Man'.

His patient had a long history of various debilitating symptoms, including obsessional thoughts, impulses to do things that he knew were harmful or disgusting, and compulsions to perform idiosyncratic rituals. Dealing with these symptoms had seriously affected his everyday life, making decision-making tortuous and resulting in chronic procrastination that led him to take 10 years to obtain a legal qualification and spend many years trying to decide if he should marry or not. The obsessional thoughts included the worry that his father and the young woman he was attracted to might die and a constant fight against the impulse to take a razor and cut his own throat. For a time, he became convinced that the young woman would be horribly injured in a carriage accident caused by the carriage wheel hitting a stone in the road. Lanzer was moved to go to the road and remove a stone that the carriage might drive over, only to feel compelled to go back later and put the stone back in the very same place from where he had removed it – then to worry again and return to remove the stone in a compulsive repetitive cycle.

For Freud, these compulsions and obsessions had their root in Lanzer's early development, so he applied his technique of free association to explore his patient's childhood. Lanzer recounted that when he was six years old a governess had allowed him into her bed and he had become sexually excited. After that, at any opportunity, he had crawled beneath her dress to fondle her genitals. This had led to a strong desire to see women naked, a desire that was accompanied by very strong feelings of guilt. When Lanzer was 12, he fell in love with a girl who was unaware of his feelings and barely noticed him. He fantasized that his father would become ill and die and this would result in the girl giving him the attention he craved. Freud noticed that running through these and the many other accounts Lanzer gave of his symptoms were conflicted feelings about his loved ones. He both loved and hated the people he was close to; he wanted to protect them but harm them too.

The cruel captain

The event that led him to be referred to as the Rat Man occurred when Lanzer, who was a member of the military reserve, was called up to go on manoeuvres with his unit. When he arrived at the military base, he realized that he had lost his spectacles. While waiting for a new pair to be made in Vienna, he spent time talking to a couple of officers. An army captain with a reputation for cruelty told Lanzer a story about a torture in which the victim was laid on the ground and a pot containing rats was placed over his buttocks. Lanzer could not bring himself to make explicit to Freud what happened next and Freud had to say for him – since the rats had no other means of escape they would have to burrow through the victim's anus to escape from the pot.

As Freud spelled out the nature of the torture that Lanzer was alluding to, he noticed that a look of both horror and pleasure passed over Lanzer's face, betraying the ambivalence Lanzer felt towards his loved ones. The source of this ambivalence was un-resolved conflict resulting from his relationship with his father, which was tied up with his early sexual desires. He wanted to see naked women, but he believed that if he did so his father would die. These sexual desires could not be 'unwished', so he was always in a state of intolerable guilt. His unresolved Oedipal hatred for his father and his guilt for this hatred was pushed deeper into his unconscious, where it developed in the form of obsessions and compulsions. According to Freud's case history, the treatment of Lanzer was a complete success and after each obsessive belief and compulsion was addressed through free association it disap-peared, never to return.

LITTLE HANS: PHOBIA

The second of the 1909 case studies was 'Analysis of a Phobia in a Five-Year-Old Boy'. The little boy was given the name of Hans in the case study, but his real name was Herbert and he was the son of one of Freud's friends, Max Graf. Graf was a member of a group that came to Freud's home every Wednesday to discuss dreams, the unconscious and psychoanalysis. Freud had been asking members of this group to collect observations of the sexual life of children, so Graf had been keeping notes on his son since he was two years old. Graf had observed that Herbert took great interest in his penis, which he called his 'widdler', and he asked his parents if they had 'widdlers' too. His mother told him that she did. On seeing a cow being milked, he remarked that milk was coming out of the cow's 'widdler'.

When Herbert's mother found him touching his penis at about three-and-a-half years of age, she told him to stop and threatened to send him to the doctor to have his 'widdler' cut off. Herbert's self-stimulation and his interest in 'widdlers' was not reduced and he became increasingly curious about the anatomical differences between males and females. All the while his father was assiduously writing down Herbert's questions about 'widdlers' so that he could pass them on to Freud. But when Herbert was four and a half, Graf wrote to Freud that rather than just contributing to the observations of infantile sexuality, Herbert was now a 'case history' because he had become very anxious, telling his parents that he was scared that his mother might leave him and that if he left the house he might be bitten by horses. These fears had emerged suddenly, on a walk in the park with his nurse, when Herbert was overcome by distress and demanded that he be taken home to his mother immediately.

Over the next few days Graf talked to his son about his feelings and thoughts. On one occasion Herbert came to his parents' bedroom and asked to get in the bed so that he could be comforted by his mother. His father encouraged the boy to go back to his own room, but his wife overruled him and Herbert was allowed into the bed. The next day, Graf asked Herbert why he had wanted to spend the night with his parents. He told his father that two giraffes, a tall one and a small 'crumpled' one, had been in his bedroom and he had taken the 'crumpled' giraffe away. The large giraffe called to the 'crumpled' giraffe' to come to him but the 'crumpled giraffe' had ignored these calls. Herbert had sat down

Herbert Graf, 'Little Hans', was studied in depth by Freud. His father took extensive notes on his development from a young age.

on the 'crumpled' giraffe and, eventually, the large giraffe had stopped calling.

In a letter to Freud, Graf interpreted this fantasy in terms of the Oedipal relations between himself, Herbert and his wife, arguing that the large giraffe was himself, the father, with his 'big penis', and the 'crumpled' giraffe was Herbert's mother. In the fantasy Herbert had 'taken' his mother from his father and

by sitting on her, signalling his possession and his victory over his father. Freud agreed with Graf's interpretation of the fantasy and the source of Herbert's anxiety; Herbert's sexual attraction to his mother was becoming more intense and was threatening to

Herbert Graf related that two giraffes that had appeared in his bedroom – a large one and a 'crumpled' one.

overwhelm him. As these sexual feelings would not go away they were repressed, becoming unconscious. According to Freud, in a reply to one of Graf's letters, 'He is really a little Oedipus, who wants his father "away", done away with, in order to be alone with his beautiful mother, to sleep with her'.

The Oedipal roots of Herbert's distress were clear to Freud and Graf, but this still left the mystery of the very specific horse phobia. At this point Herbert recalled that his fear of horses had begun when he had been out with his mother and saw a horse struggling to pull a heavily laden bus but fall down, clattering noisily on the cobles as it tried to stay on its feet. The boy was sure that the horse had died before his eyes. When Max and Herbert visited Freud in his consulting rooms, Freud noticed that Max's thick moustache and spectacles were visually similar to the blinkers with sheepskin nosebands that were fitted to horses to stop them being distracted by other horses and traffic. Herbert had wished his father dead like the horse that had fallen in the street – but was now feeling guilty because he loved his father dearly. He was also terribly scared that his father would castrate him. To deal with these conflicting feelings, Herbert repressed his hatred of his father and displaced his fear of being with him onto a fear of the world outside the family home. His castration anxiety he displaced onto a fear of horses. Helping Herbert to understand that he had wished his father dead like the horse in the street, and that his terror of his father was feeding his terror of being bitten by a horse, allowed Herbert to deal with the Oedipal conflict of feeling that his father was an all-powerful rival for the possession of his mother.

DANIEL PAUL SCHREBER: A STUDY IN PARANOIA

In *Psychoanalytic Notes on an Autobiographical Account of a Case of Paranoia (Dementia Paranoides)*, published in 1911, Freud put forward a psychoanalytic interpretation of the illness of Daniel Paul Schreber (1842–1911). Schreber was born in Leipzig to an upper-class, high-achieving family. His father ran a sanatorium and Daniel and his brother Gustav both studied law and became

Daniel Paul Schreber was a judge who suffered from hypochondria and hallucinations. Freud was able to analyze Schreber only through his autobiography.

judges. In 1885, after standing for election to the German parliament, Schreber became ill and sought help from a psychiatrist, Professor Paul Flechsig (1847–1929), who diagnosed hypochondria. This was successfully treated and Schreber recovered, but eight years later, after he became Senate president of a court in Dresden, his illness recurred and became increasingly serious.

The hypochondria presented as an oversensitivity to light and sound. Schreber would sit immobile for hours on end and began to experience hallucinations and delusions. Initially he believed that he was being persecuted by Flechsig, who wanted to subject him to 'soul-murder' and to operate on his body to turn him into a woman. As his delusions developed, he believed that it was God rather than Flechsig who was persecuting him and he spent hours speaking with God directly. This delusion was then turned on its head and Schreber became convinced that God wanted to work with him to turn him into a woman, not as a cruel torture and punishment but so that he/she would be able to bear God's children and thus save the world. Schreber's physical condition deteriorated as he avoided food for long periods of time and also refused to pass faeces, resulting in serious concerns for his health.

The story of Schreber came to Freud secondhand. Freud never met him in person but read about his case in Schreber's autobiography *Memoirs of My Nervous Illness*, which Schreber wrote to prove that he was not insane and that he should be released from the psychiatric hospital.

Dora, Rat Man and Little Hans are examples of Freud's treatment of neuroses including hysteria, obsessional behaviour and phobia. According to Freud, psychoses which resulted from withdrawal from reality and the total domination of the psyche by the unconscious were not amenable to psychoanalytic treatment. Schreber's autobiographical material gave Freud the opportunity to demonstrate that psychoanalysis could be used to understand psychoses even if the technique could not be used as a treatment.

Freud's analysis of Schreber's autobiography is highly controversial, because he interprets Schreber's symptoms as the result of

A photograph of the psychiatrist Paul Fleschig at his desk in 1909.

Sergei Pankejeff was known as the 'Wolf Man' in Freud's case notes.

someone resisting homosexual impulses. Freud's analysis begins with Schreber's relationship with Flechsig. After the onset of the first illness Schreber, according to Freud, had been grateful to Flechsig for curing him of his first attack of hypochondria, but his gratitude was intertwined with an intense erotic attachment to the psychiatrist. Schreber had fallen in love with him, yet these homosexual longings were unacceptable to the middle-aged, middle-class judge and he could not cope with them. To deal with this conflict, Schreber's intense feelings of love became reversed. He now hated Fleschig just as intensely as he had loved him but struggled to account for this change, and it is here that the feelings of persecution appeared: to justify this new hatred, Schreber began to believe that Fleschig was plotting to harm him.

WOLF MAN: INFANTILE NEUROSIS

Freud presented his case study of the 'Wolf Man' in a 1918 paper entitled 'From the History of an Infantile Neurosis'. Wolf Man was Sergei Pankejeff (1886–1979), who sought treatment with Freud in February 1910 because he was finding it increasingly difficult to function; after visiting a series of psychiatrists including the famous Emil Kraeplin (1856–1926), he had been diagnosed with incurable manic-depressive insanity. Freud was to spend four-and-a-half years treating Pankejeff and early in the analysis diagnosed him as suffering from an infantile neurosis. Over the course of the treatment and over 100 pages of a case study, Freud painstakingly and systematically reconstructed the first eight years of Pankejeff's childhood development, convinced that his problems lay in his past rather than in brain degeneration.

What emerged was that according to Pankejeff his early childhood had been unremarkable. His recollection was that his parents had always told him that he was quiet and good-natured until he was about three and a half, when he became quite naughty and began to throw violent tantrums during which he screamed and could not be calmed. He also began to masturbate, for which he was severely punished by his nurse. During anal-

Der Wolf und die sieben jungen Geißlein.

Es war einmal eine alte Geiß, die hatte sieben junge Geißlein, und hatte
sie lieb, wie eine Mutter ihre Kinder liebhat. Eines Tages wollte sie
in den Wald gehen und Futter holen; da rief sie alle sieben herbei und sprach:
„Liebe Kinder, ich will hinaus in den Wald, seid auf eurer Hut vor dem

An illustration from the fairy tale The Wolf and the Seven Little Goats.
Pankejeff found this story particularly terrifying.

ysis, he remembered that at this time he had fantasies of being smacked on the penis. He also recalled that his elder sister had tormented him by making sure that he could not avoid seeing a picture of a wolf which illustrated the fairy tale 'The Wolf and the Seven Little Goats', and always scared him. On his fourth birthday, which fell at Christmas, he dreamt of wolves sitting in a tree outside his bedroom window and became terrified of them. This phobia died down, but then Pankejeff became obsessed with religion and religious ritual, praying for hours, compulsively making the sign of the cross and taking every opportunity to kiss religious icons. He was also obsessed by dung and took pleasure in cruelty to animals, searching the garden for caterpillars so that he could cut them up alive and watch them writhing.

During the course of the analysis, Freud and Pankejeff identified the dream about wolves as a key event in the development of his problems. He remembered that he had gone to bed and fallen asleep thinking about the presents lying under the Christmas tree. In the dream he woke up to see his bedroom window opening of its own accord to reveal six or seven huge white wolves with fox-like tails sitting in the tree outside. Ears pricked, the wolves were alert, staring at the little boy. Pankejeff woke terrified from the dream. After careful analysis of it and the use of free association to explore other childhood events, Pankajeff was convinced that this dream was referring to an earlier event that had been repressed.

Freud analyzed each element of the dream and concluded that it was full of imagery related to castration anxiety, with the huge fox-like tails which, according to Freud, compensated for taillessness – that is, the real tails had been chopped off and therefore referred to castration. Freud concluded that the earlier event that Pankejeff had repressed was that when he was about 18 months old, he had seen his parents having sexual intercourse, his mother on all fours with his father entering her from behind. Freud called a child observing their parents having sex as the 'primal scene' and argued that psychologically it is highly significant because the child usually sees the act of sex as an act of aggression by the father against the mother, yet it is sexually exciting and usually results in intense castration anxiety. In the dream of the wolves, the primal scene was symbolized by Pankejeff lying in bed and the whiteness of the wolf's coats was an association to his parents' underclothes and bedclothes when they were having sex.

Pankejeff underwent analysis with Freud six times a week for nine months of each year for four-and-a-half years. Pankejeff had been described as untreatable, but Freud declared him cured.

Key Points

- Between 1905 and 1918, Freud wrote up four extended case studies on his patients and a fifth study based on the autobiography of a psychiatric patient.

- The case studies provide an insight into Freud's psychoanalytic practice and illustrate how he used his method to treat hysteria, obsessional neurosis, phobia and infantile neurosis.

- Ranging from the relatively simple (Little Hans) to the complex and convoluted (Wolf Man), the studies demonstrate the importance of infantile sexuality for understanding adult dysfunction and show how free association and dream analysis could be used to reveal unconscious infantile wishes.

CHAPTER 6
The methodology of psychoanalysis

Freud's famous case studies discussed in the previous chapter give an insight into the process of psychoanalysis, but they mix case history, description, theory and analysis based on the treatment of patients that range from the relatively brief to the long term; Freud met Little Hans only once, but treated the Wolf Man for more than four years. The case histories are also rather short on the practical details of how to conduct a psychoanalysis of a patient, since they were written to give the reader an overall picture of psychoanalytic thinking rather than as practical guides to psychoanalysis. In this chapter we shall turn to the methodology of psychoanalysis more explicitly, first to examine the theoretical assumptions underlying Freud's methodology and then to discuss his specific advice on psychoanalytic technique.

INTROSPECTION VERSUS PSYCHOANALYSIS

From the end of the 1880s, German academic psychologists such as Wilhelm Wundt (1832–1920), who was usually referred to in psychology textbooks as the first 'scientific' psychologist, were embracing tightly controlled introspection as the method to investigate the structure of mental phenomena. In 1907 Wundt laid down four rules for truly scientific introspection. These rules were:

1 The observer must as far as possible be in a position to determine for himself the occurrence of the event to be observed.

2 The observer must be in a state of the utmost concentration of attention to observe the phenomena and to follow them in their course.

3 In order to safeguard the results, every observation must be capable of being repeated a number of times under similar circumstances.

4 The conditions under which the phenomenon occurs must be ascertained by variation of the accompanying circumstances, and, when they are ascertained, they must be regularly changed in the appropriately varied experiments.

(From Wundt, W. [1907]. Über Ausfrageexperimente und über die Methoden zur Psychologie des Denkens, *Psychologische Studien*, 3, 301–360.)

According to Wundt, if these methodological rules were followed, then the mind was 'transparent', so it was possible to observe mental life directly and on this basis build a scientific and objective psychology. To follow these rules was by no means an easy task, and Wundt insisted that observation was carried out by carefully trained assistants whose reports were accepted only after they had practised introspection for tens or even hundreds of hours.

Freud's starting point as a psychologist was very different. After he returned from his stay in Paris studying with Charcot, he became a clinician and was wedded to the clinical method for the rest of his career. Instead of specially trained assistants who were in total control of their self-observations (a scientific method of introspection), Freud was dealing with clients who were coming to see him because they were distressed and *not* fully in control of themselves. The goal of the clinical session was very much one of treatment, and the development of theory was for Freud something that should take place from experience in the clinical setting. Clearly Wundt would not have allowed any of Freud's patients to participate in his experiments and Freud's methods would have had no place in his approach to psychology. A more profound difference between Wundt and Freud was the key lesson that Freud had taken from treating patients: introspection was limited as a method for investigating the mind. After spending many hours working as a clinical neurologist, his firmest empirical conclusion was that the basic problem his patients were suffering from was a

Wilhelm Wundt (1832–1920) was one of the first 'scientific' psychologists.

lack of access to early childhood memories, no matter how hard they concentrated. These memories were available through the process of psychoanalysis and were the result of the application of the techniques of free association (see p.70). We shall now return to the method of free association again in order to highlight how Freud's use of the method and his commitment to the existence of the unconscious was a radical starting point for psychoanalysis.

THE METHOD OF FREE ASSOCIATION

When Freud began to use the method of free association, it was not entirely new. In the late 1870s, while taking a leisurely walk down Pall Mall in London, Sir Francis Galton, a key figure in the development of psychometric methods, had noticed that the 300 or so objects he was aware of on his way elicited memories of things and people from different periods of his life. Later he carried out experiments using lists of words and timing how long it took each word to elicit a memory. From these, he found that associations from early childhood were more common than recent memories, suggesting that the early years have a special significance in laying down memories that are forgotten under many layers of subsequent memories. In his *Inquiries into Human Faculty and its Development* (1883) Galton was convinced that his experiments and observations suggested that there was 'a strata of mental operations wholly below the level of consciousness', but he made no attempt to describe or investigate the nature of these operations.

For Galton, the method of free association could bring to light connections between people, objects and events of which the respondent was currently unaware by 'digging' through the layers. In *The Interpretation of Dreams*, Freud argued that early memories may be forgotten, not because they have been 'overwritten' by more recent memories but because of an active process of repression that works to keep them from awareness. The seduction theory holds that these repressed memories are of sexual assault; according to psychoanalysis, the memories are of infantile

The psychologist Francis Galton (1822–1911) was one of the first to recognize the power of the method of free association.

sexual wishes. The key point is that in his first topography, de-scribed in *The Interpretation of Dreams*, Freud conceived the psyche as being made up of the unconscious, pre-conscious and conscious thoughts, with repression acting like a process of censorship. In the next chapter we shall see how in his second topography Freud built on the first to present a developmental and structural model comprising the id, ego and superego in constantly changing relationships, with censorship crucial to maintaining balance between these different agencies.

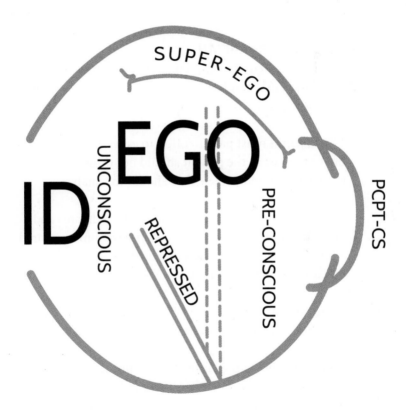

Freud's diagram of the psyche, showing the id, ego and super-ego, from his New Introductory Lectures on Psycho-Analysis *(1933). The term 'PCPT-CS refers to the perception-consciousness system.*

In the context of Freud's discovery of repression the method of free association took on a new importance. The starting point of the process was not random, such as Galton walking down the street, nor a word list as used by the students of Wundt and by Jung; in the clinical setting it was a dream, a parapraxese (a slip of the tongue such as referring to 'Fraud' rather than 'Freud') or a troubling symptom. The fundamental rule that a patient (analysand) had to agree to was that they would say what they thought or felt and not hold back, even if what came to consciousness was unpleasant or shocking, nonsense or ridiculous, trivial or irrelevant.

THE ROLE OF THE PHYSICIAN

In a 1912 article entitled 'Recommendations to Physicians Practising Psycho-analysis', Freud set out a series of nine recommendations that should be followed by a psychoanalyst:

> 1 The analyst must pay attention to everything the patient says; just as the patient should not think anything too trivial for analysis, neither should the analyst.

> 2 The analyst must write down accounts of dreams and important dates – for example, when symptoms appeared – but should not make notes during the session because this will distract the analyst from listening to the patient.

> 3 The goal of analysis is treatment, not scientific rigour, so do not use this as a reason for keeping notes.

> 4 Since psychoanalysis is based on clinical experience and evidence, the analyst must be careful. It is the evidence in front of the analyst that is important rather than theory.

5 Just as a surgeon has to set aside sympathy in order to complete an operation that causes pain to his or her patient, so should the psychoanalyst.

6 The analyst must at all times be receptive and attentive to the patient.

7 The analyst must not reveal his or her feeling or thoughts to the patient; the analyst must be like a mirror to the patient.

8 The patient isn't a 'project' for the analyst to or invest in. The goal is to remove symptoms.

9 The analyst should not discuss psychoanalytic theory with the patient, nor with the patient's family.

THE COUCH

The traditional set-up of a psychoanalytic session is for the patient to be lying on a couch with the analyst positioned behind it, out of sight. Freud first established this arrangement when he was using the hypnotic method to treat patients. Once he invented psychoanalysis, he soon found that the set-up was useful for reducing distractions; because the patients could not see his facial expressions they had to concentrate on their own thoughts and feelings rather than trying to interpret Freud's attitude. He also remarked that he would have found it very tiring to be under the scrutiny of a series of patients throughout the day, which might involve up to eight hours of clinical appointments. Freud also believed that the couch aided in the process of transference, which was to become a key tool of psychoanalysis.

RESISTANCE

Psychoanalysis was born out of Freud's discoveries of his patients' resistance to treatment; it appeared that they simply didn't want to accept his help and be cured. This resistance could take the form of repression, which was the process of censorship that prevented overwhelming memories from reaching consciousness, and of transference, in which the patient resisted the psycho-

analyst by reacting to them on the basis of previous relationships; this might result in the patient rejecting or accepting interpretations, not because of their merit, but because the patient was living out old relationships. Freud, however, increasingly saw

A photograph of Sigmund Freud's study early in the 20th century, showing the couch he used to treat patients.

transference as something that could be used as a tool rather than an obstacle to treatment.

The other types of resistance that Freud was to identify included what he called the 'gain from illness', which includes the relief of keeping the repressed memory at bay and the secondary gain from the sympathy and care that being ill might invoke from others. In the second topography, as we shall see in the next chapter, Freud identified these forms of resistance with the ego. He also identified a need to repeat which he associated with the id, and which results in the patient not being able to give up symptoms even though the unconscious basis of those symptoms has been discovered and at a rational level accepted by the patient. Freud linked this form of resistance to what he called 'working through' which, like transference, he considered an aid to treatment because the patient's repetition of symptoms and the repetition of their interpretations led to their gradual wearing down and removal. The fifth type of resistance that Freud identified was a need for punishment and the experience of guilt, which would eventually be associated with the actions of the superego.

TRANSFERENCE

In the case history of Dora, Freud came to the conclusion that Dora was not treating him as an independent and disinterested physician who had her treatment and her best interests at heart, but as the proxy of her father and Herr K. Freud was frustrated at this outcome and considered the projection of previous relationships onto the clinical relationship as an obstacle to psychoanalysis. He quickly realized that this transference cropped up in every analysis. When he asked his patients to free associate about a dream or symptom, they would often stop, instead of following the fundamental rule and reporting the thoughts that were 'falling out' of their minds. When he challenged them about why they had stopped, they might report that they had embarrassing thoughts about Freud; they might want to pursue a sexual relationship with him or to subject him to violence. The goal of analysis was of course to resolve the conflicts caused by repressed infantile sexual wishes; Freud wanted to disappear from the analysis as a real person and take the role of a mirror, but his patients would not allow this to happen.

Freud became aware that during analysis the feelings and thoughts the patient has about the analyst are actually feelings about significant figures in their childhood, such as parents or siblings, which cannot be made conscious but which are revived and relived in the interaction with the analyst. So, for example, if a male child is unable to resolve Oedipal hatred for his father, this hatred might be played out by an adult in analysis as hatred of the analyst. Freud's insight that he could use these transferences as material for interpretation and that the relationship between analyst and patient must become the

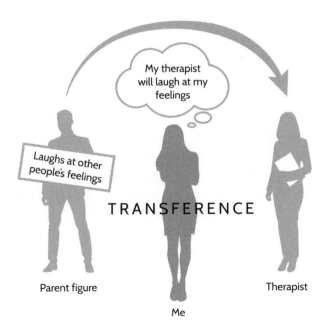

Freud discovered that an individual would often project their attitudes towards the figure being discussed on to him. He described this process as 'transference'.

main focus for treatment was his most important methodological breakthrough since *The Interpretation of Dreams.* The benefit of focusing on these transferences is that for the patient the relationship with the analyst is in the here and now, so their emotions and feelings are direct and intense even though the relationship that is being played out might be with a long-dead parent. Freud's goal of resolving infantile neuroses through the discovery of transference was thus to give him a new route to unlocking the unconscious.

As Freud explored the phenomeon of transference through the rest of his career, he began to conceive of it as a neurosis in its own right, which he called transference neurosis. This was a re-living of the original infantile neurosis, and the successful treatment of the transference neurosis, which led to the dissolving of the transference relationship with the analyst, meant that the infantile neurosis had been successfully treated.

COUNTERTRANSFERENCE

Freud was quick to exploit the phenomenon of transference and to forget his initial worry that it was an obstacle for analysis. In his guidance for physicians, he had warned against the analyst reacting to the patient in an emotional or non-objective manner. The recommendations that the analyst and patient should not see each other during analysis and that the analyst should refrain from investing in the patient beyond the goals of treatment were there to help the analyst remain objective about the nature of the clinical relationship. After the discovery of transference, the separation of the analyst and patient took on a new importance, because now the analyst was not just a mirror reflecting back to the patient the structure and contents of their unconscious conflicts; the analyst was able to make use of the distortions that were seen in the mirror by the patient and which were caused by previous relationships, so the less the patient saw and knew about the analyst, the easier it was for the patient to project these relationships on to them.

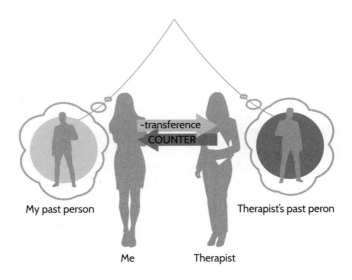

Freud realized there was the possibility for countertransference, when the analyst would project a past person of their own onto their patient.

Of course the same was true for how the analyst related to the patient. Freud recognized the possibility of countertransference, in which the analyst brings their own unresolved unconscious conflicts to the analysis and begins to treat the patient in terms of their own relationships. Freud warned analysts to be on guard for countertransference and to address it as quickly as possible. He recommended that if it became a problem for the treatment, the analyst should conduct a self-analysis or go back into analysis themselves.

HOW WAS FREUD SURE THAT PSYCHOANALYSIS WORKED?

During psychoanalysis the patient offers up dreams, slips of the tongue and symptoms for analysis. These are interpreted by the analyst and might be resisted, but if the interpretations are eventually recognized by the patient the symptoms are relieved and the patient can move on in their treatment. In the case of the Wolf Man (see p.109), Pankejeff's apparently incurable mental illness was dissolved over a period of four-and-a-half years as Freud traced his many and varied symptoms back to the infantile neurosis that lay at their root. In this slow process the key to success was Freud's correct interpretation of the latent, unconscious content underlying the material revealed through free association.

Reading the case studies is a good way to get a sense of this process, but they also highlight the difficulty of evaluating the success of Freud's methodology because it is difficult for the reader to assess his interpretations, which can appear implausible. For Freud, the veracity of the interpretations was something that was established on the couch in the clinical setting. Freud was sensitive to criticisms that the patients' acceptance or rejection of interpretations resulted in a 'Heads I win, tails you lose' situation; if the patient accepted an interpretation offered by the analyst, this proved that the interpretation was correct, but if they rejected it, that was a sign of resistance. Freud argued that was unjust and misconstrued the methodology of psychoanalysis. It was not that the psychoanalyst was always right; during the course of analysis they might offer interpretations that were incorrect or which led to blind alleys. However, as these had no effect on the patient, the interpretations dropped out of the analysis. The patient was therefore not simply open to the suggestions of the analyst but was driven by their lived experience and what felt real to them. According to Freud in his *Introductory Lectures on Psychoanalysis* (1917), 'After all, his conflicts will only be successfully solved and his resistances overcome if the anticipatory ideas he is given tally with what is real in him. Whatever in the doctor's conjectures is inaccurate drops out in the course of analysis; it has to be withdrawn and replaced by something more correct.'

As we shall see in Chapter 9, Freud's linking of the correctness of interpretations with the success of treatment has led some of his critics to argue that Freud's accounts of cures such as that of the Rat Man and Wolf Man were either false or hopelessly

INTRODUCTORY LECTURES ON PSYCHO-ANALYSIS

A COURSE OF TWENTY-EIGHT LECTURES DELIVERED AT THE UNIVERSITY OF VIENNA

BY

PROF. SIGM. FREUD, M.D., LL.D.
VIENNA

AUTHORIZED ENGLISH TRANSLATION
BY
JOAN RIVIERE

WITH A PREFACE
BY
ERNEST JONES, M.D.
President of the International Psycho-Analytical Association

LONDON : GEORGE ALLEN & UNWIN LTD.
RUSKIN HOUSE, 40 MUSEUM STREET, W.C. 1

The title page of the English translation of Freud's Introductory Lectures on Psychoanalysis. *The book consisted of 28 lectures delivered between 1915 and 1917.*

Criticisms of Freud's methods suggested that patients were put into a 'Heads I win, tails you lose' situation.

exaggerated. Furthermore, by his own criteria, if psychoanalytic treatment does not remove symptoms, then the whole edifice of psychoanalysis itself falls.

When Freud first presented psychoanalysis he was happy to describe it as a technique that recognized the existence of a dynamic unconscious and the various types of resistance, notably repression and transference, which the analyst needed to confront in order to allow the patient to recognize their own conflicting infantile wishes that were the cause of their symptoms. Free association allowed the analyst to interpret the patient's resistance and recover the patient's repressed conflicts, thus producing a cure. In the early years of the development of psychoanalysis, Freud was happy to accept anyone as a psychoanalyst who recognized the phenomena of resistance, repression and transference. In the next chapter and in Chapter 8, we shall see how Freud moved psychoanalysis beyond a form of treatment and methodology for uncovering unconscious thoughts to a theory that was wedded to infantile sexuality and, in particular, to the identification of the Oedipus complex as the heart of psychoanalysis.

Key Points

- Freud regarded the psyche as being made up of the unconscious, pre-conscious and conscious thoughts, with repression acting like a process of censorship.

- In Freud's method of free association, the patient was required to hold nothing back, no matter if it was unpleasant, trivial or apparently irrelevant.

- The analyst must pay attention to everything the patient says, following the same fundamental rules that governed the patient's free association.

- Patients might apparently not want to be cured. Their resistance might take the form of repression, transference and countertransference.

CHAPTER 7
Key psychoanalytic concepts

While *The Interpretation of Dreams* was published in 1900 to introduce Freud's key concepts of psychoanalysis, he developed and reworked these concepts over the next 30 or so years. In this chapter we shall examine what Freud considered to be the non-negotiable foundations of psychoanalysis, which was identified in an encylopaedia published in 1923 as 'the principal subject-matter of psycho-analysis and the foundation of its theory. No one who cannot accept them all should count himself a psycho-analyst.' These foundations or, as Freud referred to them, cornerstones, were the existence of unconscious processes, the theory of resistance and repression, the importance of sexuality and the existence of the Oedipus complex.

UNCONSCIOUS PROCESSES, RESISTANCE AND REPRESSION

In the first topography presented in *The Interpretation of Dreams*, Freud distinguished between different regions of the psyche, which he identified as the unconscious (UCs), preconscious (Pcs) and conscious (Cs). The conscious mind is protected from the potentially disturbing and overwhelming content of the unconscious by the process of repression. When people become ill, the mechanisms that maintain repression are breaking down and the repressed memories are returning in the form of symptoms for which the patient is seeking relief. In the process of psychoanalysis the analyst is faced with the problem that while the patient, or analysand, is seeking help, their psychic apparatus is actively repressing the very knowledge that could be used to obtain relief. During treatment the psychoanalyst inevitably faces the problem of the analysand's resistance, first in the form of repression and then through the process of transference, when the analysand cannot remember how they treated significant figures in childhood but enact their repressed behaviour with the psychoanalyst. In the case of Dora (see p.91), Freud, as we have seen, realized that by scrutinizing transference and examining the analysand's attitude to the psychoanalyst, the latter had an

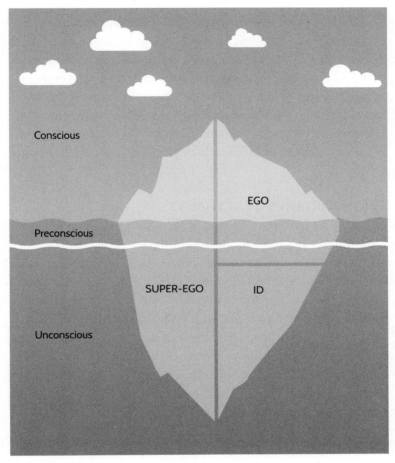

The mind can be seen as an iceberg, with the conscious mind as the area above the water, the preconscious mind as the area immediately below the water, and the unconscious making up the vast majority of the mind.

important tool for understanding the past relationships of the analysand, uncontaminated by repression and other defences.

In *Beyond the Pleasure Principle* (1920) and in other works appearing in the 1920s, Freud developed what has become known as the 'second topography'. The basic distinctions between Usc, Pcs and Cs were maintained, but instead of using the language of regions, implying different areas of the psyche, Freud turned to the language of functions or agencies and began to understand the structure of the psyche in terms of the id, ego and superego. In this new model of the psyche Freud embraced a developmental perspective explaining the sequence of the formation of these agencies during childhood and, as we shall see below, placed the Oedipus complex at the heart of his theory. But first we shall turn to Freud's concept of libido, which places sexuality at the centre of human life.

THE IMPORTANCE OF SEXUALITY

In 1871, *The Descent of Man, and Selection in Relation to Sex* by Charles Darwin (1809–82) was published. In it, Darwin applied his theory of evolution to the human race, radically changing how scientists understood what it meant to be human. Sex and reproduction became topics that they could discuss and theorize about. Freud was conversant with Darwin's theories and as a scientific naturalist believed that any account of the human psyche must be consistent with the Darwinian account of evolution. For Freud, the importance of sexuality was also revealed in his clinical work, since hysteria, which he had become so fascinated by after his visit to Paris to work with Charcot, had been understood as an illness related to the female reproductive system.

THE LIBIDO

Freud had been convinced that child sexual abuse was the cause of adult hysteria, only to reject this theory and maintain that it was caused instead by the repression of infantile sexual wishes that could no longer be contained. In this new view, the child did not suddenly become sexual at puberty but had been a sexual being since birth. Freud developed this theory of infantile sexuality over the course of his career, but it was his 1905 presentation of *Three Essays on the Theory of Sexuality* that became his most well-known statement of his views. These essays went through numerous editions, which Freud edited and amended as his views

Freud was well aware of Charles Darwin's theory of evolution and tried to apply his ideas to the workings of the human psyche.

changed and developed. Key to Freud's understanding of sexuality was the concept of libido. A term that Freud borrowed from the German psychiatrist Albert Moll (1862–1939), libido was used to refer to a specifically sexual energy that was linked to the instinct for reproduction, which Freud originally contrasted with the instinct for self-preservation; this he labelled the ego instinct.

These two instincts and the energies associated with them were often pitted against each other, with the biological imperative to reproduce fighting against the biological imperative to survive. In the 'three essays' Freud addresses sexual aberrations, infantile sexuality, the body as a site for sexual excitation and finally the transfer of the focus of sexual excitation from ones's own autoerotic excitement to another person and adult sexuality.

To this day, Freud's arguments regarding sexual aberrations remain controversial because, according to him, sexual practices that were viewed as legally and morally abhorrent were not the result of catastrophic brain degeneration but were at the outer poles of a continuum between what was considered as sexual normality and sexual perversion. Freud held that perversions such as paedophilia and zoophilia, which take children and animals respectively as their object of desire, could be understood as phenomena that were acquired during childhood and could potentially be treated. He argued that in normal sexuality, practices such as sadism and masochism were quite natural and present in all people. They became perverse only when they became the sole focus of an individual's sexual activity.

In the second essay, on infantile sexuality, Freud argued that sexuality begins in early childhood and must be understood more broadly than in terms of sexual intercourse between adults. For Freud, sexuality encompasses all activities and the pleasures derived from those activities that go beyond the satisfaction of basic physiological needs, hence the potential conflict between the sexual instinct and the self-preservation instinct; the pursuit of sexual excitation may potentially lead us into activities that override our personal safety.

To understand psychosexual development, Freud argued that the first step is to recognize that the whole of the human body is capable of becoming sexually excited; excitation is not confined to the genitals. He holds that although the whole of the body may become sexually excited, some parts are predestined, presumably as a result of evolutionary pressures, to become the particular focus for sexual excitation at different periods of physical and psychological development. These different areas of the body which become the focus of sexual excitation are called by Freud 'erogenous' or 'erotegenic' zones.

Psychosexual development

The newborn infant's contact with the world is very limited. Vision and physical coordination are relatively poor, so the primary way the infant interacts with its mother is through the mouth and the action of sucking the nipple. While the infant obtains life-preserving nutrition by this means, the very act of sucking is a source of sexual excitation in its own right. This can be observed when the infant continues sucking at the breast when no milk is forthcoming. It is at this stage that thumb sucking becomes a regularly observed phenomenon. The infant gains sexual pleasure and release from sexual excitement by the act of sucking of the thumb and there is a detachment from the self-preserving ego instinct. Freud called the period when the mouth is the principle erogenous zone 'the oral phase'. He then went on to describe how, during psychosexual development, the principal erogenous zones shifted location over time.

In his final writings on psychosexual development, Freud identified five phases. These are outlined below.

Oral phase (birth to 18 months)

The oral phase, in which the mouth, tongue and lips are the primary erogenous zone and source of sexual pleasure, is in operation between birth and about two years old. At around two there is a shift to the anal canal and anal sphincter as the primary erogenous zone. Freud notes that this is the normal course of development, but that it is possible, because of trauma or some peculiarities in the process of weaning the infant from the breast or the bottle, that the importance of the mouth as a primary erogenous zone does not subside. Freud calls this 'fixation' and argues that these disruptions in psychosexual development can be observed in adulthood in sets of characteristic patterns – so, for example, someone who is fixated at the oral phase may have an inordinate fondness for sucking a pen or pencil when stressed.

Anal phase (18 months to 3 years)
The 18-month-old child is beginning to have more control over its body and is beginning to talk. Typically, this is the time when children are 'potty trained' and learn how to control their bowel movements. The child can choose to expel or withhold faeces and in doing so can gain pleasure or be frustrated. Crucially, during potty training, the child is interacting with a caregiver and can please or frustrate them by using, or refusing to use, the potty. At this stage rudimentary social relationships are being established and the child is learning about giving into or refusing the demands of others. Fixation at this stage may take the form of compulsive tidiness or compulsive messiness, depending on whether the fixation is related to 'holding on' or 'letting go'.

Phallic phase (3 to 6 years) and the Oedipus complex
During his self-analysis Freud began to refer to the play *Oedipus Rex* by Sophocles to make sense of his love for his mother and his feelings of hostility and jealousy towards his father. He was immediately convinced that these feelings were not unique to him but were universal features of all human development. Over the next 30 years, Freud revisited and revised his account of the importance of these Oedipal feelings and published an essay in 1910, 'A Special Type of Choice Object Made by Men', in which he coined the term 'the Oedipus complex', borrowing the term 'complex' from Carl Jung to refer to an organized group of ideas

that are for the most part unconscious. To understand the dynamics of the Oedipus complex, it is useful to revisit Sophocles' account of the relationship between Oedipus, his father and his mother.

The story of Oedipus
In this Greek tragedy, King Laius and Queen Jocasta of the city of Thebes have a son. Laius consults an oracle to find out what can be expected for his son and is told that he is destined to kill his father and sleep with his mother. Laius has a servant pin the baby's feet together so that he cannot crawl and orders Jocasta to kill the baby, but she cannot bring herself to do it and asks a servant do so instead. The servant leaves the baby on a hillside to die, but he is discovered by a shepherd, who takes him to Polybus, the King of Corinth. Lacking children of his own, Polybus brings up the child himself and calls him Oedipus, or 'Swollen Foot', referring to the injury caused by pinning his feet together.

Oedipus reaches manhood and hears rumours that Polybus is not his real father. Visiting an oracle, he is told that he is destined to kill his father and sleep with his mother. Horrified, Oedipus, still believing that Polybus is his real father, leaves the kingdom and sets off for Thebes. On the way he argues with a traveller coming in the opposite direction. They fight and Oedipus kills the traveller. That traveller was King Laius and the first part of the prophecy has come true.

As Oedipus nears Thebes, he encounters the Sphinx who rules over the city. She gives travellers a riddle to solve, devouring them when they cannot answer it: what has four legs in the morning, two at midday and three at night? Oedipus gives the answer: a human being who crawls in infancy, walks on two legs in adulthood and uses a stick to support him or herself in old age. The Sphinx kills herself and Oedipus enters Thebes, where he is treated as a hero for relieving the city of its harsh ruler and is invited to marry Queen Jocasta as a reward. Thebes, however, does not prosper and a famine blights the kingdom. Oedipus is told that it is caused by the impiety of Lauis' murderer not being brought to justice. He seeks to discover who murdered Laius and, eventually, finds that he himself was the culprit. Queen Jocasta hangs herself and a bereft Oedipus uses the pins that hold Jocasta's dress together to blind himself.

A piece of Greek pottery, c. 470 BCE, shows Oedipus in conversation with the Sphinx. Freud's theory of the Oedipus Complex is one of his most well-known contributions to psychology.

In Freud's second topography, the story of Oedipus and the Oedipus complex have a crucial role in the development of adult sexuality and the formation of what Freud called the superego. At around three or four, the child takes increasing pleasure from their own genitals, discovering masturbation and also realizing there are anatomical difference between males and females. It is at this stage that Oedipal thoughts are at their height, with the child recognizing the father as a rival for the affections of the mother and disturbing feelings of jealousy and rage leading to the desire to kill the father in order to exclusively possess the mother. The

A section of Freud's manuscript notes on the Oedipus complex.

newfound recognition of the difference between male and female anatomy adds a further dimension to the conflict because the male child begins to fear emasculation (the removal of the penis and testicles), thinking that this is a fate that has already befallen females. Freud labels this fear 'castration anxiety'.

The male child, who is physically small and powerless, is in no position to challenge his father for possession of his mother, so he deals with the conflict by internalizing the prohibitions against desiring his mother and wanting to kill his father. By doing this, the child has, as it were, added an inner voice to their psychic apparatus which subsequently acts like a judge or censor. This internalized agency is the superego and is, according to Freud, the heir to the Oedipus complex.

Freud's account of the Oedipus complex and its resolution through the formation of the superego starts with the male child as the default case. Freud works out his theories of how female children negotiate the Oedipus complex in *Some Psychical Consequences of the Anatomical Distinction between the Sexes*, published in 1925. When male children discover the anatomical difference between males and females they experience intense castration anxiety which, in Freud's words, results in the Oedipus complex being 'literally smashed to pieces'. Females, on the other hand, have to come to terms with having already been 'castrated' and experience feelings of inferiority, envying males their penises, which they consider to be superior to their own external genitalia. The upshot is that female children can never satisfactorily resolve the Oedipus complex and can therefore never fully develop a superego. Feminist critics of psychoanalysis have been trenchant critics of this aspect of psychoanalytic theory, labelling it sexist and patriarchal (see p.191).

Latency: 6 years to puberty

The genital phase of development just described is characterized by Oedipal wishes that are resolved through the development of the superego. This period is marked by intense repression and

An illustration of Oedipus and Jocasta from Voltaire's Oedipus, *a play based on Sophocles' tragedy* Oedipus Rex.

A portrait of Sigmund Freud holding a cigar, c. 1921.

results in the child entering a period of latency during which sexuality sinks into the background and the child forgets the dramatic sexual excitations they have recently experienced. In this period sexual desire is seen as shameful and disgusting and energy is devoted to friends and school work.

Puberty/genital phase

In the final phase of sexual development, sexual excitations return after the period of latency. The erogenous zones which have been successively activated during the previous dozen or so years become integrated with the genitals, becoming the main source of sexual pleasure and the object of sexual excitement becoming members of the opposite sex located outside the family.

THE SECOND TOPOGRAPHY

Freud's account of psychosexual development explains adult sexuality as the result of a complex path from infancy to sexual maturity, on which the libido is satisfied in, successively, the oral, anal and genital erogenous zones. Freud links the transformation of the aims (sucking, holding on, masturbation and so forth) and objects (mouth, anal canal, genitals and so forth) with the inevitable conflicts with the life-preserving ego instincts to create an account of the developing id, ego and superego from birth to adulthood. These terms built on and superseded Freud's first topography presented in *The Interpretation of Dreams*.

In the second topography, developmentally, the unconscious is primary, with the child governed simply by pleasure. The newborn can suck or not suck and is satisfied or not satisfied. The onset of the anal phase and working through the phallic phase with the crucial negotiation of the Oedipus conflict constitutes the development of the ego. The ego powered by the instinct of self-preservation is governed by the reality principle and now these two agencies governed by different principles will inevitably come into conflict. During the phallic phase the relationship between the child and its parents or caregivers become paramount and the Oedipal wishes for the possession of the mother and jealousy of the father result, as we have seen, in the formation of the superego.

The major difference between the first and second topography was that, by the time he presented the latter in 1923 in *The Ego and the Id*, Freud had recognized that repression and resistance could have different sources and that the id, ego and superego did not map directly onto the unconscious, conscious and preconscious thoughts; there were aspects of the ego and superego that could be unconscious.

Key Points

- Having distinguished repression, resistance and transference, Freud began to understand the structure of the psyche in terms of the id, ego and superego.

- Freud presented *Three Essays on the Theory of Sexuality*, in which he addressed sexual aberrations, infantile sexuality, the body as a site for sexual excitation and the shift from sexual excitation from one's own autoerotic excitement to another person and adult sexuality.

- Freud argued that the first step to understanding psychosexual development is to recognize that the whole of the human body is capable of becoming sexually excited. He used the term 'libido' to refer to a specifically sexual energy that was linked to the instinct for reproduction.

- In the essays, he defined five phases of psychosexual development and the Oedipus complex, where the child loves the mother and feels jealousy and hostility towards the father.

CHAPTER 8
The Early Growth of the Psychoanalytic Movement

Until the publication of *The Interpretation of Dreams* in 1900, Freud discussed his ideas with his close friends, Breur and Fliess. He was making a living through his private practice as a neurologist, but he was by no means overwhelmed by patients seeking him out for treatment. When he was first developing psychoanalysis in the late 1890s he attracted some followers, including his former patients Emma Eckstein (1865–1924) and Felix Gattel (1870–1904), a German/American medical doctor who was impressed by Freud's work on aphasia. He had approached Freud to take him on as a student and stayed with the Freud family for six months in 1897. Eckstein and Gattel carried on working together for a few years, but by the turn of the new century they were not part of Freud's circle. Freud and his new science of psychoanalysis was not making a significant impact on the academic and medical scene in Vienna.

THE WEDNESDAY PSYCHOLOGICAL SOCIETY

This began to change in 1902, when Freud invited some colleagues to his home to discuss problems in the understanding of psychology. The group began to meet regularly every Wednesday evening and became known as the Wednesday Psychological Society. The first four members were Alfred Adler (1870–1937), Max Kahane (1866–1923), Rudolf Reitler (1865–1917) and Wilhelm Stekel (1868–1940). These men were all medically trained, all were Jews and all shared an interest in exporing the ideas that Freud had presented in *The Interpretation of Dreams*. More medical practitioners and also other academics and artists began to join the group, including Otto Rank (1884–1939) in 1905. Rank was not medically trained, but he impressed Freud so much that he became one of his closest aides. From 1906, he was in charge of minuting the meetings of the seminar. Another attendee of the Wednesday Psychological Society was Max Graf, father of Herbert Graf, the subject of the 'Little Hans' study of a phobia (see p.101).

A photograph of Alfred Adler and Leonhard Seif in 1925. Adler was one of the original members of the Wednesday Psychological Society.

New recruits in 1906

Until 1906, the Wednesday seminar was very much a Viennese affair. This changed when Freud's psychoanalytic writings came to the attention of Eugen Bleuler (1857–1939) and Carl Gustav Jung (1875–1961). Bleuler was professor of psychiatry at the University of Zurich and director of the internationally renowned Burghölzli Hospital in the city, and Jung his assistant director. A world-famous psychiatrist, Bleuler would coin the term schizophrenia in 1908 to replace Emil Kraepelin's earlier term of dementia praecox to categorize conditions with symptoms such as hallucinations, delusions and withdrawal from the world (see the case of Schreber, p.106). For Freud, the collaboration was both personally and professionally rewarding. It was gratifying for him that his work was being approved by such an eminent figure, and on a professional level, Bleuler was the first university professor to publicly acknowledge that psychoanalysis was a new and valuable contribution to psychiatry and psychology. Most importantly, he began to send a steady stream of his staff to Vienna to learn from Freud, and this became a source of new psychoanalysts.

Just as significant was Freud's burgeoning relationship with Jung, who was to found the Sigmund Freud Society in Zurich, later renamed

Eugen Bleuler was the director of the Burghölzi clinic in Zurich, a psychiatric hospital that was established in 1870.

as the Psychoanalytical Society of Zurich. Freud began to see Jung as an heir apparent who could lead the psychoanalytic movement after Freud's death and, as a non-Jew, would head off potential anti-Semitic accusations that psychoanalysis was a 'Jewish' science.

Carl Jung was Bleuler's assistant director at the Burghölzi clinic. He eventually broke off from Freud's psychoanalytic approach to form his own, equally influential methodology.

Through the influence of the Swiss psychiatrists, Freud's approach to the unconscious began to attract international interest, bringing others into his growing psychoanalytic community. The German Karl Abraham (1877–1925) and the German/Russian

Max Eitingon (1881–1943) were sent by Bleuler from his Zurich hospital; Sándor Ferenczi (1873–1933) came from Hungary in 1909.

An engraving of the Burghölzi clinic in Zurich in 1790.

DISCUSSIONS OF THE VIENNA
PSYCHOANALYTIC SOCIETY—1910

ON SUICIDE

With Particular Reference to Suicide among Young Students

With contributions by

ALFRED ADLER, SIGMUND FREUD,
JOSEF K. FRIEDJUNG, KARL MOLITOR,
DAVID ERNST OPPENHEIM,
RUDOLF REITLER, J. [ISIDOR] SADGER,
WILHELM STEKEL

Edited by

PAUL FRIEDMAN, M.D., Ph.D.

INTERNATIONAL UNIVERSITIES PRESS, INC.
New York, 1967

The 'On Suicide' pamphlet published by the Vienna Psychoanalytic Society in 1910.

VIENNESE PSYCHOANALYTIC SOCIETY

By 1908, a new generation of experts in the field of psychiatry was taking an interest in the study of psychoanalysis. The Wednesday Psychological Society was becoming too narrow in scope and the seminar became formalized as the Viennese Psychoanalytic Society in 1908 – the same year that the First Congress for Freudian Psychoanalysis was held in Salzburg. There the Welsh neurologist and psychoanalyst Ernest Jones (1879–1958), who was to become Freud's official biographer, was introduced to Freud by Jung. There too Freud described the case of the Rat Man. Perhaps most important was the launch of a dedicated psychoanalytic journal, *Jahrbuch für psychoanalytische und psychopathologische Forschungen* (Annals of Psychoanalytic and Psychopathological Research), edited by Jung and founded by Freud and Bleuler. It meant that psychoanalysts would not have to submit articles to journals edited by unsympathetic psychiatrists or psychologists, nor would they need to explain psychoanalytic terms from first principles in every paper that they submitted for publication.

FREUD IN THE UNITED STATES

In 1909, G. Stanley Hall (1846–1924), President of Clark College in Massachusetts, was looking for ways to celebrate the 20th anniversary of the founding of the college. The first president of the American Psychology Society in 1892, Hall had a deep interest in child development and wanted someone controversial and dynamic to visit the college. He invited Freud who, somewhat reluctantly, travelled to the United States with Jung and Ferenczi. At Clark College, he gave five lectures in one week in September, speaking German (at this time the international language of psychology). They were later translated and published in *The American Journal of Psychology* in 1910.

Freud's trip to the United States was short but influential. The Austrian-born Abraham Arden Brill (1874–1948), who

Sigmund Freud and several other psychoanalysts at Clark College, Massachussetts in 1909, including Franz Boas and A. A. Brill.

had been the first translator of Freud into English, met Freud at Clark and went on to found the New York Psychoanalytic Society in 1911. At more or less the same time, the International Psychoanalytic Association was founded, with Jung as president and headquarters in Zurich. At this time, Switzerland rather than Vienna was becoming the centre for psychoanalysis.

A group photograph at the International Psychoanalytic Congress of 1911.

SCHISMS

The story so far has been one of expansion. In the first decade of the 20th century, psychoanalysis began to attract increasing numbers of medical doctors and academics, and Freud's publications were reaching wider audiences in both the German- and English-speaking worlds. However, all was not well in Freud's circle and in a very short period some of the key figures who had helped him to develop psychoanalysis left the fold.

The first to go, in 1911, was Alfred Adler. Always an independent thinker, Adler believed that human development was driven by social relationships broader than the Oedipal relationships of father, mother and child and that social class must be taken into account in any explanation of human functioning. After he broke with Freud he developed his own school of 'individual psychology' and used the concept of the inferiority complex rather than libido to understand development. Wilhelm Stekel was the next to leave, in 1912, after relations with Freud soured when the latter refused to discuss his firm belief that masturbation after childhood was inherently harmful, leading to weakness and actual neurosis. Stekel argued that masturbation was not in itself harmful and it was the result of feelings of shame and guilt imposed by society that were the problem.

THE BREAK WITH BLEULER

Freud's association with Bleuler had proved to be highly valuable in terms of growing psychoanalysis as a new science, resulting in more students and the establishment of associations and journals to provide a setting for them to meet and publish their work. In all of this work, Bleuler was the link to academic psychology. He was, however, becoming increasingly frustrated by how psychoanalysis was developing as a science and an institution. Bleuler felt that psychoanalysis could make an important contribution to psychiatry and psychology, but he viewed it as one scientific approach among many. Freud, on the other hand, was increasingly seeing psychoanalysis as a competitor to psychiatry and psychology and began to demand that his central concepts should not be challenged. Bleuler began to resent that psychoanalysis was being presented in all or nothing terms and worried that it was becoming more like a religious sect than a science.

Bleuler left the International Psychoanalytic Association in 1911 and broke the last institutional link with Freud in 1913, when he stepped down from the editorship (held jointly with Freud) of the *Psychoanalytic Year Book*. With the departure of Bleuler, the first and last link with psychiatry and academic psychology was lost and psychoanalysis was left to develop independently of the Zurich hospital and university.

THE BREAK WITH JUNG

While the break with Bleuler was important for the development of psychoanalysis as an institution, the break with Jung was more personal and emotional for Freud. Jung had quickly become fully part of his closest circle and Freud had intended that Jung would be the permanent president of the International Psychoanalytic Association. However, when Jung first came into contact with Freud he was already a successful scientist with his own publications behind him. He was always an independent thinker, not willing to accept arguments simply on the basis of precedent and authority. According to Jung, the dispute with Freud was the latter's insistence that the interpretation of dreams rested on the principle that dreams presented a manifest content that could be analyzed in order to expose unconscious infantile sexual wishes; a dream was a compromise between the unacceptable forces of the unconscious being resisted by the ego in order to protect the individual from psychological distress. Jung's understanding of dreams was very different, regarding them not as compromises but as messages we receive about what it is to be human. By understanding these messages, an individual could be helped in times of crisis to attain self-realization, which Jung thought of as deeper understanding of oneself. The messages are drawn from a collective rather than individual conscious and Jung saw part of his work as uncovering the contents of the collective unconscious by examining the stories and imagery found in different religious traditions and spiritual practices, ranging from Christianity to alchemy and ancient Egyptian and Indian systems.

This profound disagreement on the nature of dreams was too much for Freud and Jung and in 1913, with much bitterness, the two men ended their friendship and their professional collaborations. In a matter of just over a decade Freud had managed to develop psychoanalysis dramatically but also to alienate most of his earliest and closest collaborators.

THE SECRET COMMITTEE

The arguments and schisms in Freud's inner circle worried him. His fledgling psychoanalysis was in danger of fragmenting and he was concerned that what he considered to be the concepts of psychoanalysis – Oedipus complex, infantile sexuality and so forth – were losing their centrality and that there was a growth of 'depth psychologies' which drew on the techniques of free association and resistance but did not, as far as he was concerned, count as psychoanalysis proper. Ernest Jones offered a solution to this problem. He proposed handpicking a group of psychoanalysts,

A photograph of Freud and the other members of the 'Seven Rings Committee'.

all analyzed by Freud, who would be committed to upholding Freud's account of psychoanalysis without deviation and to working to keep psychoanalysts together and prevent further schisms. On the death of Freud, this committee would appoint a successor as leader of the psychoanalytic movement and ensure that this leader kept the torch of Freud's theories alive.

Freud jumped at this suggestion since it meant that what he saw as his personal creation of psychoanalysis would be maintained, unchanging, after his death. The group picked as members of this secret committee were Jones, Sándor Ferenczi, Max Eitingon, Hanns Sachs, Otto Rank and Karl Abraham and in 1913 they met in Freud's home, where Freud presented them with gold rings set with gems engraved with images from Roman mythology. These rings were symbolic of their allegiance to Freud, who wore a ring with a head of Jupiter. The formation of the committee did not entirely stop disputes breaking out in the inner circle and Rank left in 1924 after yet another dispute concerning the status of the Oedipus complex, to be replaced by Anna Freud, Sigmund's daughter. The committee was disbanded in 1927 and its role was taken over by the International Psychoanalytic Association.

BECOMING A PSYCHOANALYST

While Freud was a medical doctor, as were the early members of the Wednesday seminar, Freud did not believe that medical training was an essential qualification to be a psychoanalyst. Both Otto Rank and Theodor Reik became notable psychoanalysts without medical backgrounds. Indeed, Freud was concerned that making medical training a prerequisite for becoming a psychoanalyst would ensure that psychoanalysis was swallowed by medicine, and he believed that an interest in psychology and an openness to psychoanalytic thinking was far more important than attending a medical school.

This issue became of more concern when Reik was taken to court for in 1926 for 'quackery' – that is, practising medicine without adequate training. Freud sprang to Reik's defence and wrote *The Question of Lay Analysis*, in which he defended the expertise of non-medically trained psychoanalysts treating neurotic disorders. Within the psychoanalytic community the debate rumbled on. In general the Europeans supported lay analysis, but in the United States there was a strong feeling that psychoanalysts should be trained medical doctors and preferably trained psychiatrists too. Theodor Reik had emigrated to the United States by this time, and was told that he could not join the American Psychoanalytic Association. Freud's position was that good psychoanalytic training was more important than good medical training, but in some ways this was just as contentious an issue because the training of psychoanalysts had varied very widely since Freud had carried out his own self-analysis in the late 1890s.

PSYCHOANALYTIC TRAINING

Freud initially believed that his founding of psychoanalysis on the basis of his own self-analysis could prove a model for others. However, the discovery of the importance of transference and the practical difficulties that analysts faced when dealing with resistance convinced Freud that self-analysis was not enough and that training to become a psychoanalyst was essential. The first psychoanalysts were students and friends of Freud, whom he trained in a rather informal and haphazard manner – for example, Max Graf received instruction on how to treat his son by letter. Some of these early followers of Freud who joined the Wednesday seminar became famous psychoanalysts in their own right and several former patients went on to practise as psychoanalysts themselves, but in general it was enough to be analyzed, however briefly or informally, by Freud to qualify someone to become a psychoanalyst without any further training or supervision.

Given that Jung was to leave the psychoanalytic community in an atmosphere of such bitterness and recrimination after he could no longer accept some of the key principles of psychoanalysis, it is perhaps ironic that it was Jung who insisted that training should be formalized. Max Eitingon was instrumental in this. He had undergone five weeks of analysis with Freud in 1908 and in 1920 had founded the Berlin Psychoanalytic Clinic and Institute. There he designed what became known as the Berlin or Eitingon, or Eitingon-Freud, model of training analysis. In this model, those wishing to become a practising psychoanalyst were required to undergo a 'training analysis' by an experienced psychoanalyst, whether or not they had any specific

The Russian doctor and psychoanalyst Max Eitingon helped develop the method for training analysts.

neuroses that need addressing. They were also required to attend lectures and seminars on psychoanalytic theory and practice and, finally, conduct clinical work themselves under the close supervision of an experienced psychoanalyst. This was known as a 'control analysis'. Eitingon's model became the standard approach to training psychoanalysts for much of the 20th century.

THE DEATH OF FREUD

By the mid-1930s psychoanalysis had developed from the conversations between Freud and his close associates Breuer and Fliess to a worldwide institution backed up with international associations, congresses, specialist journals and formal training courses. Freud's theories about the unconscious, repression, infantile sexuality and the Oedipus complex were reaching a wide audience and his books were bestsellers. Nevertheless, Freud's life was imperilled by political events in Germany and Austria and by his increasingly poor health. The rise of National Socialism with its virulent anti-Semitism was a threat to Freud on both a personal and institutional level. The Nazi party came to power in Germany in 1933 and annexed Austria in 1938. As a prominent Jew, albeit an avowed atheist, he came under attack. His passport was taken away and his freedom of movement curtailed; his books were publicly burned as examples of decadent celebrations of sexual perversion, and psychoanalysis as an institution came under attack as a 'Jewish' science. Meanwhile, Freud's life-long adherence to smoking had led to the development of cancer of the mouth and, despite numerous operations, the cancer could not be stopped.

In 1938, after the intervention of prominent scientists from around the world and the payment of a large 'fine', Freud was allowed to leave Vienna and travel to London, where he set up home at 20 Maresfield Gardens in Hampstead. His cancer was now terminal and just 15 months later, he died, in September 1939, aged 83. The death of Freud marked the end of classical psychoanalysis, but by no means the end of Freud's ideas; after his death psychoanalysis came under new scrutiny and his ideas spread beyond outside the clinic.

Freud's final home at 20 Maresfield Gardens is now the site of the Freud Museum, London.

Key Points

- In a matter of 20 years, Freud became a world figure and his small circle of friends and colleagues developed into an institution with associations all over Europe and the United States.

- Psychoanalysis, which had been introduced in *The Interpretation of Dreams*, had become a recognized therapy delivered by trained professional practitioners.

- The theory of psychoanalysis was refined and elaborated by Freud, who was firmly in control of any conceptual developments and jealously guarded the central concepts of the Oedipus complex and infantile sexuality. Any deviation resulted in expulsion from the psychoanalysis societies.

CHAPTER 9

Conflicts and Controversies

Up to this point, the focus of the book has been to present the development of psychoanalysis on Freud's own terms in order to show how psychoanalytic concepts developed and formed as a coherent whole. In this chapter we shall consider some of the criticisms that have been levelled at both psychoanalytic theory and Freud the man, mainly from outside the psychoanalytic community.

THE BREAK WITH ACADEMIC PSYCHOLOGY AND PSYCHIATRY

By the end of 1913, the collaborative relationship between Freud and the psychiatrist Eugene Bleuler was over and the development of psychoanalysis occurred outside the university and psychiatric systems. Within the university setting, different schools of psychology came and went. Wilhelm Wundt developed an approach to psychology based on introspection carried out by specially trained participants under rigorously controlled conditions. This approach was challenged by the so-called behaviourists, who considered that studying conscious experience could never be made sufficiently objective and who attempted to build a new psychology based on publicly observable stimuli and responses. In 1913, the American John B. Watson (1878–1958) presented his 'behaviourist manifesto' in which the rejection of consciousness and introspection from psychology was made explicit and the goals of psychology were set as the prediction and control of behaviour. This behavioural approach to psychology was further developed in the 1930s by B. F. Skinner (1904–90) who, in his *Behavior of Organisms* (1938), argued that studying consciousness and mental life had been a blind alley that had led nowhere; he held that it should be replaced by a psychology that studied the relationship between the motor behaviour of an organism, whether it was a rat or a human, and its environmental consequences.

In Europe, the tight limits placed by Wundt on the use of introspection were relaxed and, for example, the Gestalt

John Broadus Watson was the leader of the behaviourist movement, beginning the divergence between academic psychology and Freud's psychoanalysis.

Max Wertheimer was one of the founders of Gestalt psychology, which argued that our experiences are always part of a dynamic whole.

psychologists led by Max Wertheimer (1880–1943) conducted research into the principles that govern perception and productive thinking. The Gestalt psychologists started with the processes experienced by all people and they showed no particular interest in psychopathology. While they were interested in the dynamics of mental life, they had no explicit role for censorship and resistance in their account of conscious experience. For the most part these developing forms of psychology had little or no interaction with psychoanalysts or with psychoanalytic theory, unless to reject it out of hand or, at best, treat it as an interesting source of hypotheses.

THE SCIENTIFIC STATUS OF PSYCHOANALYSIS

The different kinds of academic psychology (psychology taught and researched in the university) were identified by their practitioners as scientific disciplines. For the behaviourists, science was a matter of objectivity which they understood as the rejection of any concepts that involved conscious experience in their explanations of behaviour. The Gestalt psychologists considered themselves scientists because their psychology was based on demonstrations of psychological experiences that were open to anyone. Of course, Freud regarded himself as a scientist. In his career he had made relatively important contributions to the fields of biology, medicine and neurology and he saw psychoanalysis as a continuation of this scientific work. In *Project for a Scientific Psychology*, he had attempted to tie the psychoanalytic concepts of the unconscious, primary processes, the ego and repression directly to the neuronal structure of the brain, hoping to unify neurology, psychology and physics. In the end he was forced to abandon this project when he could not satisfactorily ground clinical observations with the neuron doctrine, but he never abandoned his belief that psychoanalysis was a science and that it would one day be shown in some way to be compatible with our understanding of the brain.

For the rest of his career, Freud carefully distinguished be-

Karl Popper was one of the leading philosophers of science of the 20th century, but began his intellectual adventure by studying psychology.

tween psychoanalysis considered as a clinical theory grounded in empirical research and what he called his metapsychology, which was conceived as a generalized theory of the mind which could be altered as new clinical insights were discovered. He considered the clinical theory to be validated on the couch, when the process of free association, dream analysis and the examination of parapraxes led the patient to recognize the unconscious forces that were producing their symptoms, resulting in the symptoms disappearing. Since Freud was confident in his identity as a scientist, he had no need for the approval of academic psychologists or much interest in their empirical research. Psychoanalysis and academic psychology thus developed in different directions with little or no points of contact and with no cause for dispute, as there was little overlap in their domains of interest.

AN EXPLANATION OF EVERYTHING AND NOTHING

It was not from academic psychology directly that the scientific status of psychoanalysis was first challenged. Karl Popper (1902–94), who is now recognized as one of the most eminent and influential philosophers of science of the 20th century, began his career by studying psychology in the late 1910s, but he never held an academic position as a psychologist. He took a PhD at the University of Vienna with the eminent developmental and cognitive psychologist Karl Bühler (1879–1963). As well as conducting research on cognition, Popper also spent time working at a clinic for troubled working-class children run by Alfred Adler, one of the original members of Freud's Wednesday Society, who had broken with Freud in 1911 after disagreements over the centrality of infantile sexuality and the effect of social context on development. Adler had gone on to found his own school of individual psychology, which is now best remembered for introducing the concept of the 'inferiority complex'.

These were intellectually exciting times in Vienna, and Popper and his friends spent many hours discussing the work of

A portrait of Albert Einstein in 1905. Popper identified that there was a clear difference between Einstein's theories and those of thinkers like Marx and Freud.

Freud, Adler and Karl Marx (1818–83) as well the recent theories of Albert Einstein (1879–1955), whose theory of special relativity was published in 1905, followed by his theory of general relativity in 1915. Popper noticed that his friends who were fully committed to psychoanalysis, Adlerian individual psychology or Marxism found evidence for their favourite theories all around them. This puzzled Popper, who could not help feeling that there was an important difference between the theories of Freud, Adler and Marx on the one hand and Einstein on the other. To try to illuminate this difference, Popper conducted a thought experiment; he imagined how a psychoanalyst and an Adlerian might explain the actions of a man who pushes a child into a lake to try to drown him or her. For the psychoanalyst, this aggressive act would be explained in terms of Oedipal conflicts, while the Adlerian would interpret it as the man's effort to deal with an inferiority complex by proving, either to himself or others, that he dared to commit a crime.

If a second man dived into the river to save the child, the psychoanalyst would likely explain this as the sublimation of Oedipal drives in which aggressive urges are acted out in terms of socially acceptable actions. For the Adlerian the life-saving act would again result from an inferiority complex, as this heroic action would prove to others and himself that he dared to save the child. In this thought experiment Popper concluded that both the Adlerian and psychoanalytic theories could explain these antisocial and altruistic acts. Popper's deduction was that psychoanalysis and Adlerian individual psychology were so general and their concepts so flexible that they could explain *any* human behaviour.

CONJECTURES AND REFUTATIONS

Einstein's theories of relativity, on the other hand, generated very specific hypotheses. One prediction was that light rays from stars passing by the sun would be bent by the sun's gravitational field. The degree of deviation could be calculated and then the actual deviation measured. If there was no deviation, or the amount of deviation calculated from the theory did not match the observed deviation, then the theory of relativity was simply wrong. In 1919 Arthur Eddington went on an expedition to the west coast of Africa and, measuring the deviation of the light rays during a solar eclipse, he found that the amount of deviation was as predicted from the theory of relativity.

For Popper, this was the perfect example of what demarcated science from non-science and pressed home the difference between the theory of relativity and psychoanalysis and Adlerian psychology in that the theory of relativity was constructed so that it could be refuted by observation. Popper went on to argue that psychoanalysis and Adlerian individual psychology (and also Marxism) were not sciences because any observation could be fitted into their conceptual framework and it was not clear what evidence could ever bring about a psycho-analyst giving up on the Oedipus complex and the existence of the unconscious. Popper's observations about the nature of psychoanalytic theory were made during Freud's lifetime but were not widely disseminated until 20 years after his death when, in 1963, Popper published *Conjectures and Refutations: The Growth of Scientific Knowledge* and his argument became widely used by critics of psychoanalysis.

Ernest Gellner (1925–95), an anthropologist and social theorist, was highly influenced by Popper and in *The Psychoanalytic Movement* (1985) he agreed with Popper's view of why psychoanalysis was not a true science. He then went on to explore from a sociological perspective how and why psycho-analysis had been so successful if it was merely a pseudo-science; after all, tens of thousands of people experiencing distress had sought treatment from the many hundreds of trained psychoanalysts. He concluded that the all-encompassing conceptual scheme that made psychoanalysis unscientific was what made it attractive and satisfying for people who were looking to make sense of their lives. Compared to the psychology of the behaviourists (which understood what it was to be human in terms of chains of stimuli and responses) or the emerging cognitive psychology which developed in the 1950s and 1960s (and understood what it was to be human in terms of the inputs and outputs of computers), psychoanalysis with the conflicting id, ego and superego was so much richer. Also, of course, Freud addressed human sexuality directly and, curiously, this was a topic that was missing from most academic psychology.

Gellner also noted that the investment in time and money to train to be a psychoanalyst and the time and money that patients invested in their treatment engendered a commitment by both practitioners and patients which was difficult to break. For Gellner, in the final analysis psychoanalysis should be understood not as a science but as an institution that was structured like a religion with the psychoanalyst playing the role of the priest. Gellner's problem with psychoanalysis was that it was presented as a science, not as a faith or a life style, and promised effective treatment of distress; but it was not based on scientific evidence because, Gellner argued following Popper, no evidence could ever be provided that would result in a psychoanalyst giving up their practice. At best, psycho-analysis might have a placebo effect, with no direct therapeutic value from the identification of repressed wishes but making patients feel better about themselves because they were taken seriously and given attention by a respected analyst. At worst, psychoanalysis was a waste of time and effort and prevented distressed people from seeking help from psychiatrists and clinical psychologists – whose treatment was based on evidence that could be evaluated.

THE IMPORTANCE OF THE CLINICAL THEORY

The effectiveness of psychoanalysis became a salient issue, first in the United Kingdom, then in the United States in the 1940s and '50s, when advocates of the developing field of clinical psych–

ology began to compete with psychoanalysis for recognition and financial support. A key event was the visit of Hans Eysenck (1916–97) to the United States in 1949, to speak to clinical experts and gather information that he could use to design the curriculum for the first course of clinical psychology in the United Kingdom. Eysenck, a German-born psychologist who had made his career in the United Kingdom and developed influential theories of personality, travelled the length and breadth of the United States. After attending lectures and seminars and immersing himself in the clinical literature, he became increasingly critical of psychoanalysis as a treatment of neuroses and other disorders. He believed that any evidence for the success of psychoanalytic treatment was anecdotal at best and relied on the testimony of the psychoanalyst and/or the patient rather than any independent criteria of effectiveness.

For Freud, the testimony of the psychoanalyst and the patient was adequate evidence – if the psychoanalyst's interpretations were accurate, they were accepted by the patient and the patient's symptoms were removed. But Eysenck argued that independent evidence was necessary and in 1953 he published a paper in the *Journal of Counselling Psychology* on the effects of psychotherapy, in which he concluded that psychoanalysis and psychotherapy were no more effective than chance at treating mental health problems and that in the studies he had reviewed, two out of three patients spontaneously recovered with no treatment of any kind. He argued that if psychoanalytic treatment were to be deemed to be an effective treatment of neurosis, the outcomes of treatment must be better than the rate of spontaneous recovery. He found that no such study had been carried out.

At this point, Eysenck was content to point to the lack of evidence of the effectiveness of psychoanalysis to argue that clinical psychologists should look to behaviourism and personality theories to design their curricula. Later, in his *Decline and Fall of the Freudian Empire* (1985), Eysenck made an all-out attack on Freud and psychoanalysis, arguing that psychoanalysis was not a science and should be abandoned wholesale.

Hans Eysenck and his wife Sybil. Eysenck pioneered work on the nature of intelligence and personality.

Agreeing with Eysenck's critique of the effectiveness of psycho-analytic treatment, a philosopher Adolf Grünbaum (1923 – 2018) argued contrary to Popper, that psychoanalysis was a science and could be empirically tested. He argued that Freud's justification for the scientific respectability of his clinical method was based on what he dubbed Freud's 'tally argument' – that in the course of analysis the patient's Oedipal conflicts would be successfully resolved only if the interpretations offered to the patient by the analyst tallied with the patient's experiences; if the interpretations offered by the analyst were deemed inaccurate or irrelevant by the patient they would drop out of the analysis.

The key issue here is that the psychoanalytic process of re-vealing to the patient the repressed infantile wishes that had led in later life to neuroses and obsessional behaviour was the only way to achieve a lasting cure. If a treatment removed the symptoms but did not deal with the repressed wishes then, according to psychoanalytic theory, it would be expected that new symptoms would develop in place of the symptoms that had been removed. It is by the patient recognizing their unconscious wishes through the process of interpretation that the cure is achieved. Grünbaum argued that if Freud was right, then spontaneous remission or treatments that did not address unconscious conflicts were im-possible. Since there was evidence that patients could be cured by other methods and that patients often spontaneously recover, psychoanalytic theory was falsified and the theory and treatment should be abandoned.

FREUD RE-EVALUATED AFTER HIS DEATH

The critiques of psychoanalysis by Popper, Grünbaum and Eysenck focused on the status of psychoanalysis as a theory and the effectiveness of psychoanalysis as a treatment of distress. These initial critiques implied that Freud's philosophy of science was faulty but did not attack the integrity of Sigmund Freud as a scientist. From the 1980s to the present time, the integrity of Freud has come under attack: for these critics, psychoanalysis is not just judged as a false theory but as an institution built on, essentially, ambition and fraud. Before turning to these arguments, we shall look at the new histories of psychoanalysis that brought in a new understanding of the development of Freud's thinking.

NEW HISTORIES OF PSYCHOANALYSIS

Between 1953 and 1974 James Strachey (1887–1967) oversaw the publication of *The Standard Edition of the Complete Psychological Works of Sigmund Freud*, which ran to 24 volumes, giving scholars the opportunity to grasp the breadth of Freud's work. Also in the 1950s, Ernest Jones published a three-volume official biography of Freud. Often criticized as being flattering and uncritical, Jones's biography presented a narrative of Freud as a tortured genius who had made startling and original discoveries that owed nothing to others. After Freud's death new material began to be made available which challenged Jones's narrative, in particular Freud's considerable correspondence, both personal (to his wife Martha and to his childhood friends) and professional (to his early collaborators, including Jung and Ferenczi and to members of the 'secret committee'). Of particular interest were Freud's letters to Fliess. In 1937 these were put on the market and bought by Marie Bonaparte (1882–1962), a supporter of Freud. Freud wanted them destroyed but she kept them, and the complete letters were finally published in 1985.

The new availability of biographical material stimulated research into the historiography of psychoanalysis and the publication of new, more critical biographies. In 1970, in *The Discovery of the Unconscious: The History and Evolution of Dynamic Psychiatry*, Henri Ellenberger (1905–93) showed that Freud's account of the unconscious was not as original as Ernest Jones had suggested but was a continuation of ideas that had their roots in German philosophy and French psychiatry. Almost a decade later, in 1979, Frank Sulloway (1947–) published his highly influential biography, *Freud: Biologist of the Mind*, which also stressed the continu-

Marie Bonaparte purchased Freud's correspondence with Fliess, and these were finally published in 1985.

Betty Friedan delivered a devastating feminist critique to Freud's psychoanalysis in her book The Feminine Mystique.

ity of Freud's ideas with those of earlier thinkers and with his own work in biology and neurology.

In *The Second Sex*, published in 1949, the French philosopher and feminist Simone de Beauvoir (1908–86) took Freud to task for defining femininity in terms of a deviation of the male libido – a deficit of a penis, rather than as an intrinsic feminine sexuality.

Simone de Beauvoir was a leading French philosopher and one of the most prominent feminists. She fiercely criticized Freud's analysis for its apparent sexism.

This critique was taken up again by Betty Friedan (1921–2006) in *The Feminine Mystique,* published in 1963, where she argued that psychoanalysis supported a patriarchal system of domination of men over women and led a backlash against psychoanalysis. But in the 1980s the so-called 'Freud Wars' took the methodological and feminist critiques to a different level. Two of the most significant moves in this war were the publication of Frederick Crews' articles, 'Analysis Terminable' in the journal *Commentary* in 1980, and 'the Unknown Freud' in *The New York Review* in 1993. Crews (1933–), a professor of English, began his career sympathetic to Freud and psychoanalysis and, indeed, used psychoanalytic theories as a tool of literary criticism. However, he became increasingly antagonistic to psychoanalysis not only as a means of literary criticism but also as a method of treatment. Initially influenced by Grunbaum's critique, he became convinced that psychoanalysis was a menace; on a cultural and social level it presented a skewed account of what it means to be human and for the individual paying for psychoanalytic treatment it was a waste of time and money. Throughout the 1980s and to the present day, Crews' criticisms of Freud have become more trenchant. In 2017, he published *Freud: The Making of an Illusion,* in which he claimed that Freud's use of cocaine was much greater than Freud admitted in his writings and that this had led to him producing what for Crews was a grandiose theory, backed up by accounts of case histories that were more fabrication and exaggeration than careful scientific description and analysis.

Jeffrey Masson (1941–), an academic who began his career studying the ancient Indo-European language Sanskrit, retrained as a psychoanalyst. He became a confidante of Kurt Eissler (1908–99), who had founded and directed the Sigmund Freud Archives, which contained all of Freud's papers that he had left after his death and letters and writings which had been subsequently collected. Eissler appointed Masson as secretary of the archives and allowed him access to Freud's unpublished papers. In the *The Assault on Truth: Freud's Suppression of the Seduction*

Frederick Crews has cast doubts on the reliability of Freud's case studies and suggested that Freud was more dependent on cocaine than he admitted.

Theory, published in 1984, Masson accused Freud of abandoning the seduction theory which proposed that child sexual abuse was the cause of hysteria because the reception of the seduction theory had been on the whole negative; Freud's ambitions for fame and recognition were so powerful that he was happy to shift the onus away from parents and carers whom the child was accusing of abuse and argue that it was the children themselves, with their infantile sexual urges powered by their powerful libidos, who were wishing for these sexual acts to be true. For Masson this was, in effect, a betrayal of the children who had been abused.

Masson's account of Freud's retraction of the seduction theory has been disputed. Freud took some years to publish his formal retraction, which perhaps suggests that he was embarrassed to admit that he had changed his mind. Freud had always acknowledged that some, if not many, of his patients had been abused by parents, nurses, siblings and servants; his argument was that this was not the case for all of them. For Freud, the existence of one child who had repressed sexual infantile wishes concerning an adult in childhood demonstrated that the seduction theory was wrong.

Key Points

- Freud's critics such as Karl Popper and Ernest Gellner have argued that psychoanalysis is not a science and its pretentions to scientific status are ill founded.

- Other critics, including Adolf Grünbaum, have argued that psychoanalysis is a science but it is a science that is not supported on firm evidence and should be rejected.

- Hans Eysenck's work on evaluating the effectiveness of psychoanalysis has been influential, setting clinical psychology down a road which has been, on the whole, anti-psychoanalytic.

- The feminist critiques of psychoanalysis are, in effect, also critiques of the scientific status of psychoanalysis since they argue that Freud, with his discovery of the Oedipus complex and his difficulty of conceptualizing the psychosexual development of females, was simply repeating in his theorizing the patriarchal social organization of the late 19th-century society to which he belonged.

- According to Jeffrey Masson, Freud's attachment to patriarchal thinking was so strong that he was prepared to say that children were mistaken in their accounts of being sexually abused in order to have his theory accepted. These criticisms and others resulted in the 'Freud Wars' of the 1980s and '90s. Today these controversies are still unresolved, with battle lines firmly entrenched and positions staunchly defended.

CHAPTER 10
Freud outside the clinic

After Freud's visit to Charcot in 1885, his focus moved from the laboratory to the consulting room and the clinical method became his prime tool for understanding the structure of the mind. However, he was not content to confine his theorizing to the consulting room and his ambitions were always wider than inventing a technique for treating hysteria or obsessional neuroses. Freud

The front page of Imago *magazine, 1915-16.*

wanted psychoanalysis to contribute to our understanding of art, cultural, religion and politics. This ambition was demonstrated in 1912 when, along with Hanns Sachs and Otto Rank, he founded the magazine *Imago* to provide a forum for the discussion of psychoanalytic theory applied to the humanities, arts and social sciences. After the Nazi takeover of Austria in 1939, the journal was renamed *American Imago* and moved to the United States, where it is published to this day. Freud published many of his non-clinical works in the magazine in a series of papers employing psychoanalysis as a method of art and literary criticism, including discussions of the works of the Russian author Fyodor Dostoevsky (1821–81) and the artistic and scientific development of Leonardo da Vinci (1452–1519).

Freud's interest in politics and current affairs and his ambition to make an impact on culture and society were reflected in a series of papers and books, starting from around the mid-1900s and continuing to the end of his life in 1939. In 1908 he published '"Civilized" Sexual Morality and Modern Nervous Illness', and drew attention to a fundamental antagonism between human instincts and civilization, arguing that society could survive only if sexual instincts were repressed or their energy was channelled into socially acceptable pursuits such as work and art. This was to be a theme that Freud returned to repeatedly for the rest of his life, and he became increasingly pessimistic about whether this antagonism between instinct and civilization could ever be successfully resolved. In his accounts of it, Freud saw the status of religion as an important theoretical and practical battleground because for him, religion was a key cultural achievement and represented a necessary phase in the development of any civilization.

THE DEVELOPMENT OF CIVILIZATION

Freud accepted the belief, commonly held in the late 19th and early 20th century, that the development of civilizations was an orderly process leading from so-called 'primitive' or 'savage' forms of social organization to the complex, highly differentiated and culturally rich forms of social organization found in modern industrial societies. This process affected not only the development of institutions such as law and government, but also styles of thinking. The historical shifts from 'primitive' societies to 'advanced' societies was associated with a move from magical and animistic thinking via the invention of organized religions to modern scientific thinking. Freud's contribution to the de-

bate was to argue that psychoanalytic concepts could be used to explain these shifts and could contribute to our understanding of religion in modern society.

Sigmund Freud contemplates a Javanese figurine on his desk, 1937. He increasingly tried to use psychoanalysis to understand the development of societies.

Herbert Spencer believed that the cognitive development of a child could be extrapolated to understand the cognitive development of the whole human species.

RECAPITULATION THEORY AND EVIDENCE FROM ETHNOGRAPHY

Since it was obviously impossible to go back in time and observe the first attempts at social organization and their subsequent developments, these accounts of social progressive were purely speculative. To bolster them, theorists drew on 'recapitulation' theory, proposed in biology by Ernst Haeckel (1834–1919), who argued that the history of the development of a whole species can be seen in the changes that an individual fertilized ovum goes through up until birth. The English social thinker Herbert Spencer (1820–1903) made a similar point about learning, believing that the intellectual development of a child, from concrete thinking to abstract thinking, followed the same developmental path as the development of human knowledge, so by observing the cognitive development of a child one could find the whole history of the cognitive development of the species. Freud made a similar claim, arguing that the psychosexual development of a child from infancy to adulthood mapped onto the development of civilization and, since Freud's theory of psychosexual development was also a theory of the development of psychopathology, his theory could be used to diagnose and potentially treat the problems of civilization.

RELIGION AND OBSESSIONAL NEUROSES

Freud first explicitly and directly addressed religious topics in his 1907 paper 'Obsessive Actions and Religious Practices'. In this, he pointed to the similarities between obsessional neurosis and religious practice. Obsessional neurosis, an illness characterized by extreme distress caused by constant feelings of guilt and anxiety and a compulsion to repeat actions that, to an outside observer, made no sense, was typified by the Rat Man, Ernst Lanzer, who suffered from obsessional impulses to harm himself and thoughts about his loved ones being tortured by rats. Freud cured Lanzer by uncovering his unresolved wishes to harm his father and the intolerable guilt these wishes caused him to feel – that is, the

Christ Crucified *(1632) by Diego Velázquez. Freud argued that religion, and particularly Christianity, existed to offer comfort for adherents in the face of a sense of helplessness.*

experience of ambivalence (see p.101). In 'Obsessive Actions and Religious Practices', Freud argued that following religious practices and rituals could also be understood in terms of ambivalence. Obsessive neurotics and religious practitioners both felt guilty if they did not complete their rituals and resisted interruption, carrying out their rituals with complete conscientiousness; nevertheless, the rituals were always accompanied by feelings of guilt. The neurotic renounced their awful thoughts and the religious practitioner renounced their sin. The difference was that there was more variability in neurotics' rituals, which were idiosyncratic, whereas the religious rituals were public, shared by other people, and involved symbolism that was understood by all the co-religionists.

In this first major discussion of religion, Freud concluded that 'One might describe neurosis as individual religiosity and religion as a universal obsessional neurosis.' He came back to religious beliefs over the next 30 years and maintained to the end his view on the remarkable similarities between religious practice and obsessional neuroses.

TOTEM AND TABOO

The first edition of Freud's new journal *Imago* published four essays that were released in book form in 1913 as *Totem and Taboo: Some Points of Agreement between the Mental Lives of Savages and Neurotics*. In this book he followed up his ideas that religious people were akin to obsessional neurotics and presented an account of the birth of totemism as a primitive religion and the first step toward morality and civilization.

In the first essay of *Totem and Taboo*, which Freud calls 'The Horror of Incest', he describes the social and religious organization of Australian aboriginal peoples, whom he describes as 'miserable savages'. This system is based on 'totems'. The totems are often animals, objects or symbols and serve to identify and unite groups of people. Though the people may be 'miserable savages', the totemic system is highly organized and very strict. It prevents sexual relations not just between the nuclear family (which we in modern societies label as incest), but also sexual relations between members of the extended family where there are no direct blood ties and the tie is simply membership of the same totem group. Freud draws the reader's attention to the fact that our modern

industrial societies are more sexually permissive than those of the Australian aborigines. The prohibition or taboo against having sex with members of the same totemic group is extended beyond physical intercourse and members are not allowed to touch or even look at members of the opposite sex who share the same

An Australian Aboriginal ceremony from the early 20th century. Freud's Totem and Taboo *focused on the nature of Aboriginal society.*

totem. For Freud, these strict taboos are highly noteworthy because they suggest that incest for the aboriginal groups has a significance that goes beyond the avoidance of potential genetic abnormalities. (For the most part, this is what drives modern concerns about, say, cousin marriage.) Freud draws the conclusion that the strength of these taboos about the regulation of sexual relationships suggests these beliefs are in need of psychoanalytic explanation.

In the second essay, 'Taboo and Emotional Ambivalence', Freud draws on ethnographies of Polynesian islanders to argue that, just as obsessional neurotics are trying to deal with deeply troubling feelings of love and hate for their parents, 'primitive' people are in a similar predicament. Drawing on *Obsessive Actions and Religious Practices*, he argues that in totemic societies the inevitable ambivalence that children feel for their parents and group members feel for their leaders is dealt with collectively by the projection of unacceptable hating of the totem itself. The totem, becomes, as it were, a stand-in for the hatred of all authority figures which displaces the hatred away from concrete individuals to the totem. In the case of Little Hans, the boy's hatred of his much-loved father (the classic state of ambivalence) was dealt with by Hans through the displacement of his negative feelings and impulses from his father to horses, producing Little Hans's equine phobia (see p.101).

In the third essay, 'Animism, Magic and the Omnipotence of Thought', Freud draws further parallels with obsessional neuroses and 'primitive' thinking. Obsessional neurotics are in a constant state of anxiety because they believe their terrible thoughts can bring about real events. The Rat Man's unconscious wishes to harm his father by subjecting him to the rat torture could be prevented only by his completion of his various rituals. These rituals had no real causal effect in the world but, in the grip of the obsessional neurosis, there was no possibility of challenging the Rat Man's beliefs.

In the fourth essay, 'The Return of Totemism in Childhood', Freud brings the themes of totemism, taboos and obsessional neuroses together to propose a theory of the origin of totemism and thus a theory of the founding of primitive religion and the first steps to civilization. He starts with Charles Darwin's suggestion made in *The Descent of Man and Selection in Relation to Sex*, published in 1871, that the first social organization comprised a strong male who had gathered a harem of females whom he alone was allowed to impregnate. When male children reached puberty they would be ejected from the group to fend for themselves, losing the protection of their father and the love of their mother. If these young men wanted to breed they would have to individually challenge the leader of a 'horde', kill him and take over leadership.

Freud goes on to tell the story of what happened to the 'primal horde' when the ejected young men united to kill their all-powerful father and, in perhaps the first religious feast, got together as a group to eat him in order to take on his powers and to symbolically share the responsibility of the act of parricide which they had just committed. The sons were then in a position to sexually possess all the females in the horde. However, after the satisfaction of killing their father came feelings of guilt and grief because their father was gone forever, and he had protected and cared for them when they were children. Collectively the sons had to deal with these feelings of ambivalence, and they did so by honouring their father, elevating him to the status of a god, identifying him and representing him symbolically with an animal, which became their shared totem. This totem was a constant reminder of their primal crime which must never be repeated, and also of the protection they had received from their father.

The situation was not yet stable because the brothers' sexual desire for their mothers and sisters was still present, but now, no longer regulated by their father, the young men were faced with the problem of how to manage it. They could fight each other and one son could take over the role of the dead father, but the violence would be bloody and there could be repeated challenges for leadership of the group, leading to constant conflict. Collectively the sons agreed to renounce the sexual interest in their mothers and sisters which had motivated their original parricide, and to avoid sex with anyone who was identified with their father's totem. This account, according to Freud, explained the transition from the primal horde governed by the power of the father to an organization based on shared identity and shared prohibitions organized around the totem, and formed a social structure where taboos held sway rather than the exercise of raw violence. The sons were able to regulate their sexual impulses and live together because they had renounced their sexual interest in their mothers. For Freud, this was the first step leading to more complex religions and more nuanced ideas of morality – a step that was crucial and was taken because of the fundamental desire to kill one's father and sexually possess one's mother, which is of course the Oedipal structure that Freud put at the heart of psychosexual development and which he found in all of his patients.

THE DEATH INSTINCT

In his first account of psychosexual development, Freud contrasted the sexual instincts and libido with the life-preserving ego instincts. By the early 1920s Freud began to question this distinction. From 1914 to 1918, World War I had brought death and destruction to Europe and Freud was quick to diagnose the frailty and failure of civilization. During the treatment of war veterans, who had experienced terrible traumas during battle, Freud found that many had a compulsion to repeat and relive painful behaviours and experiences. He was particularly troubled by his patients who suffered from recurrent dreams reproducing the traumatic events they had experienced in battle. This could not be readily understood in terms of the fulfilment of wishes, which Freud had identified in *The Interpretation of Dreams* as the key to dream interpretation. It seemed that his patients often recalled and repeated actions that offered no possibility of pleasure or even the deferral of pleasure to avoid pain. These experiences were simply destructive.

This resulted in Freud rethinking his basic theory of instincts, and in *Beyond the Pleasure Principle*, published in 1920, he grouped the sexual and ego instincts together as the 'life instinct' and contrasted them with what he called the 'death instinct'. For Freud, the death instinct was a result of all organisms aiming to reduce tension and excitation and return to their pre-living, inorganic state. Freud never mentioned Thanatos in print, but, according to his biographer Ernest Jones, in conversation he referred to the death instinct as Thanatos, named after the ancient Greek god of death, and to the life instincts as Eros, the Greek god of love and sex. Towards the end of his life, Freud became increasingly convinced that the evidence from psychoanalysis was that Thanatos was real and that all humans had a drive towards self-annihilation as well as drives towards sexual reproduction and self-preservation. Before the reconceptualization of his instinct theory, Freud had believed that aggression was the result of conflicts between the sex and self-preserving instincts. After the introduction of Thanatos to his conceptual

Freud described the death instinct as Thanatos, *the name for the ancient Greek god of death.*

213

Romain Rolland was a French essayist who criticized Freud's The Future of an Illusion *for dismissing religious feeling too easily.*

scheme, Freud believed that when this destructive instinct was turned outwards to others, and away from oneself as its object, the result was aggression. Taking up his investigations into the development of religions and civilization in *The Future of an Illusion* (1927) and *Civilization and its Discontents* (1930), Freud realized that civilization had to withstand the forces of sexual and selfish, self-preserving instincts and also our fundamental instinct for destruction.

THE FUTURE OF AN ILLUSION

In *The Future of an Illusion*, published in 1927, Freud turned his attention to the cultural role of religious beliefs in modern society, and found religion wanting. In this book he diagnosed religion as a universal obsessional neurosis and, in developmental terms, childish and infantile. He suggested that religion, the illusion of the title, should be replaced by an orientation towards reality which might well be unsettling and difficult, but preferable to the denial of reality.

Freud began his argument against religion by pointing out that the instinctual drives already described threaten the processes of civilization. Civilizations can protect themselves from these instinctual urges by inventing moral standards that teach renunciation of sex and violence and promote art and professional work as more suitable outlets for these energies. However, Freud argued that the masses are lazy, unintelligent and hostile to these moral standards; it is necessary to offer them more direct compensation for accepting the renunciation of their instincts. This compensation comes in the form of religion. In *Totem and Taboo* Freud had described the birth of totemic religions; in *The Future of an Illusion*, he addressed the development of monotheistic religions and Christianity in particular. As a monotheistic religion which posits the existence of an all-powerful and loving 'father', Christianity offers its adherents a way of experiencing comfort and solace by satisfying the helplessness and powerlessness they had experienced since infancy. Religion was the vehicle for fulfilling infantile wishes and was therefore an illusion, just as Anna Freud's dream of eating strawberries, described in Chapter 4, was an illusion that satisfied her wish to eat real strawberries which had been denied to her by her nurse.

CIVILIZATION AND ITS DISCONTENTS

Freud developed these ideas further in *Civilization and Its Discontents*, published in 1930. He was dissatisfied with *The Future of an Illusion*, considering it to be the least successful of his books, and now he elaborated his criticisms of religion and brought sharply into focus the role that guilt plays in the maintenance of civilization, concluding that the costs of civilization are very high and make happiness an unachievable goal for most people. At the end of the book he leaves the reader wondering if members of so-called primitive societies are not happier than those living in so-called advanced civilizations.

One influential criticism of Freud's thesis presented in *The Future of an Illusion* was by Romain Rolland (1866–1944). Rolland, a Nobel Prize-winning novelist, agreed that the practice of organized religion was childish but he questioned whether religious feeling should also be summarily dismissed, arguing that there existed what he described as an 'oceanic' feeling of unlimited connection to the universe and that it was this feeling upon which organized religions had constructed an illusory superstructure. Rolland argued that the 'oceanic' feeling was real and offered the possibility of connection with other people. In *Civilization and Its Discontents*, Freud rejects Rolland's argument and reiterates his view that religion is a childish phenomenon. The 'oceanic' feeling that Roland identified is simply the longing for protection and the fulfilment of a wish for comfort and belonging; it cannot be the source of a genuine connection with others and is simply another aspect of infantile psychology.

Freud goes on to identify the sources of human unhappiness in our bodies which are destined to deteriorate and break down, the impersonal power and relentlessness of nature, before which we are helpless and, finally, the struggles we face in maintaining interpersonal relations with others. These struggles puzzle Freud because civilization, he reasons, should make living with others less painful but seems to increase our unhappiness.

To understand this chronic unhappiness, Freud argued that civilization is the product of the fundamental conflict between life and death instincts. In his account of individual development, Freud explained the formation of the superego through the process of taking on and internalizing the characteristics of the parent of the same gender – that is, internalizing authority. With the introduction of the death instincts we now have the problem of dealing with our aggressive instincts. Freud argues that these are also internalized so that the human predicament is to develop an increasingly strict superego that grows from the internalization of authority and the internalization of aggression *against* authority. The result is increasing feelings of guilt which are repressed and are expressed in increasing levels of discontent and unhappiness. The paradox of civilization is that as civilization works to control and manage our instincts (in order to protect us from irrational and dangerous desires), so the superego becomes stronger and we are punished the more, not just for acting on our instincts but for our wishes to do so. The more an individual takes on the values of a civilization and accepts its authority, the more miserable they become.

FREUD ON RELIGION AND CIVILIZATION

Freud's works on religion and civilization are attempts to challenge the religious world view. Freud was an atheist who believed that religious beliefs had played a role in the development of civilization but that they had outlived their usefulness. According to Freud, as civilization progressed it became increasingly necessary to control instinctive behaviour. Moral imperatives to renounce instincts have limited effects, so societies seized upon religious practices because these offered to fulfil wishes of completeness and comfort in the face of a cold universe, in which the powers of humans against nature and against each other were limited. Freud considered the consolations of religion to be illusory and advised that they should be given up and a scientific world view be embraced. Towards the end of his life, his hopes for human happiness were dimmed and he advised his readers to accept that to be human was to balance conflicts between life and death, Eros and Thanatos, and that no fundamental resolution could ever be found.

Key Points

- In 1912 Freud cofounds the magazine Imago to provide a forum for the discussion of psychoanalytic theory applied to the humanities, arts and social sciences.

- In *Totem and Taboo* Freud makes a link between the psychological developmental of the child and the development of society.

- In the early 1920s Freud revisits his theory of instincts and introduces the concept of the Death Instinct (Thanatos) which is opposed by the Life Instinct (Eros)

- By the end of his life Freud was pessimistic about the future of civilization arguing that civilization came with a personal cost which made human happiness difficult or impossible.

CHAPTER 11

Current evaluations of Freud and psychoanalysis

In this book the focus has been on what is often referred to in the literature as 'classical theory', referring to the key concepts and body of work that Freud himself would recognize as indispensable to the psychoanalytic approach. After Freud's death, psychoanalysis developed in different directions. In the United Kingdom, Freud's daughter Anna Freud (1895–1982), drawing on her 1936 book *The Ego and the Mechanisms of Defense*, led the Ego Psychology School of psychoanalysis, which focused psychoanalytic theory and treatment on the ego's adaptation to the environment. Melanie Klein (1882–1960) took psychoanalysis in a different direction and founded the Kleinian or Object Relations School of Psychoanalysis. In contrast to Freud himself, Klein and the Kleinians conceptualized development less in terms of instincts and the conflicts that resulted from satisfying them and more in terms of the child's need to relate to objects (for example, the mother and the breast) and the development of psychic structures through the processes of introjection and projection, resulting in a complex set of internalized representations of objects and relations to objects. Klein stressed the importance

Freud's daughter Anna became a significant psychoanalyst in her own right.

of very early infantile experiences, arguing that the first year of life was more important for subsequent development than the rest of childhood put together.

Famously, Anna Freud and Melanie Klein clashed in the 1940s over Klein's contention that the super-ego was present during this first year of life. Donald Winnicott (1896–1971) led the so-called Middle or Independent Group of psychoanalysts who tried to steer a path between the Anna Freudians and Kleinians by embracing a more pragmatic approach to theory and refusing to be drawn into ideological debates.

A photograph of Melanie Klein, c. 1927. She specialized in the psychoanalysis of children and established the Object Relations School.

In France, Jacques Lacan (1901–81) took psychoanalysis in a very different direction and founded the Structuralist or Lacanian School, arguing that it was necessary to 'return to Freud'. At the same time he drew on philosophical and methodological ideas taken from linguistics and structuralism, coining the terms 'The Imaginary', 'The Symbolic' and 'The Real' to refer to different levels of psychic phenomena which are necessary to conceptualize our position in the natural and social world.

These are just examples of the different ways in which psychoanalysis developed after Freud's death. The literature on these schools of psychoanalysis is now as large, or even larger, than that on Freud's classical theory and to do any justice to the complexity of their reworkings of Freud's central ideas would require a book-length monograph for each of them. They are the schools of psychoanalysis which still identify Freud and his body of work as their starting point. Jung, who made an early break from Freud,

223

Jacques Lacan, a French psychoanalyst, argued for a return to Freud's principles and methods.

founded his own highly influential school of analytical psychology, which although it rejects some of Freud's key ideas does share a family resemblance and history with psychoanalysis. What we can take away from the different directions that psychoanalysis went in after the death of Freud is that psychoanalysis is not a body of theory and methodology that has remained frozen in time; it continues to be developed by psychoanalysts.

THE PROGRESS OF PSYCHOLOGY AND PSYCHIATRY

The changes in psychology and psychiatry since Freud's death have been more dramatic. In the 1930s and '40s, psychology was in the grip of behaviourism, which rejected explanations that alluded to mental states and subjective experiences. Today psychology has taken a 'cognitive' turn which embraces the mental states and, in particular, the concept of mental representation. In many ways modern cognitive psychology is more in sympathy with psychoanalysis, but there are limits to any reconciliation. Cognitive psychology is concerned with non-conscious process, but in general it has no place for Freud's dynamic theory of mind, which conceptualized the mind in terms of conflicting forces and the relatively independent structural agencies of the id, ego and superego. An understanding of a cognitive unconscious is not at this time part of mainstream cognitive psychology and psychoanalysis still has not got a firm foothold in university psychology departments.

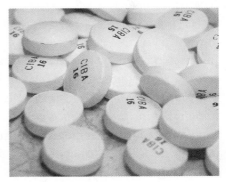

The situation of psychoanalysis with respect to psychiatry and clinical psychology is uneasy. The diagnostic categories that Freud used to classify his patients, includ-

Ritalin tablets. Since the 1950s, the preference has been to treat mental health issues with psychoactive drugs.

Aaron Beck, known as the 'father of cognitive therapy', focused on removing harmful thoughts rather than searching for childhood traumas.

ing hysteria and obsessional neuroses, are no longer used in psychiatric diagnoses. Over the last half century, the *Diagnostic and Statistical Manual of Mental Disorders (DSM) and the International Statistical Classification of Diseases and Related Health Problems* (ICD) have removed references to psychoanalytic terms and theoretical constructs so that psychiatric diagnosis today completely bypasses psychoanalysis, as does the treatment of psychiatric disorders. In the 1950s, the development of new psychoactive classes of drugs resulted in their becoming the treatment of most psychiatric disorders.

In the 1950s, Hans Eysenck's argument for clinical psychology as an explicit alternative to psychoanalysis focused on behavioural techniques to treat psychiatric distress. In the 1970s, ideas taken from psychologists who rejected the psychoanalytic concepts of repression and resistance, such as Albert Ellis (1913–2007) and Aaron Beck (1921–), focused treatment on the removal of unhelpful or self-sabotaging thoughts rather than the causes of those

The American psychologist Carl Rogers developed the approach of Client Centred Therapy.

thoughts in early infantile experience. These techniques have been found to be effective for the treatment of many forms of distress and, allied with Eysenck's behavioural therapy, have been amalgamated to form Cognitive Behavioural Therapy (CBT). Today the United Kingdom's National Institute for Health and Clinical Excellence (NICE) recommends not psychoanalytic treatment but CBT for anxiety disorders, depression, obsessive compulsive disorder (OCD), schizophrenia and psychosis and bipolar disorder.

PSYCHOANALYSIS TODAY

The importance of psychoanalysis as a way of understanding and treating psychiatric disorders has waned since the death of Freud; CBT and psychoactive drugs are much more likely to be used. While psychoanalysis is still available, it is more usually paid for by the patient rather than a national health service or private health insurance. However, while psychoanalytic ideas have been disappearing from psychiatry and clinical psychology, there has been a rise in the so-called psychotherapies. These draw on some of Freud's concepts such as the importance of early childhood experiences, unconscious processes and repression, but they reject the full psychoanalytic treatment involving free association, dream analysis and a commitment to analysis that may go on for months or even perhaps years. Instead, they generally offer shorter and more specific problem-based therapy and often draw on multiple approaches to understanding mental distress. Practitioners may describe their treatment as 'integrative' and they will be happy to mix psychoanalytic concepts with concepts drawn from other psychological approaches such as the Client Centred Therapy of Carl Rogers (1902–87), which explicitly rejects the conflict model proposed by Freud. Freud was quick to expel any of his followers who deviated from his core concepts and methods, so it is unlikely that he would have been happy that psychoanalysis was being 'diluted' or offered in a shortened form. Nevertheless, the psychotherapies do offer a home for psychoanalytically informed treatment if not the full treatment itself.

PSYCHOANALYSIS AND THE POLITICAL DISCOURSE

Freud was pessimistic about the future of civilization, believing it to be a source of increasing unhappiness rather than a solution to human problems. For him, religion was a childish illusion that offered temporary solace but no long-term answer to the management of life and death instincts. His account of the human condition in *The Future of an Illusion and Civilization and its Discontents* found an audience not just with the psychoanalysts and the interested general public but with social theorists. In the 1930s and 1940s, attempts were made to build bridges with the work of Karl Marx by members of the Frankfurt School, while in his 1955 work *Eros and Civilization: A Philosophical Inquiry into Freud*, Herbert Marcuse (1898–1979) took as his starting point *Civilization and its Discontents* and accepted Freud's account of civilization as a source of guilt and repressive forces but denied that this was inevitable. Instead, he argued that Eros could defeat

Thanatos and a new non-repressive society could be built. Marcuse's book was a bestseller and his ideas went on to influence political thinkers in the United States and Europe. Later political thinkers have attempted to link Marx and Freud and, in Europe, Marx and the particular version of Freud presented by Lacan and his Structuralist School. While these attempts are outside the main currents of political discourse, they are still influential – for example through the work of Slavoj Žižek (1949–) who presented in *The Sublime Object of Ideology* (1989) a critique of postmodernism based on a psychoanalytic theory of ideology.

THE SPAN OF FREUD'S WORK

Fitting Sigmund Freud's life and theories into a 'nutshell' is a difficult task, for Freud's ideas defy simplification and easy summarizing. This is partly on account of Freud's prodigious output – the standard edition of his published writings runs to 24 volumes – but also because he was an interdisciplinary thinker, covering topics as diverse as the biology of fish, the effects of cocaine, hypnosis and child sexual assault. After the invention of psychoanalysis, Freud developed a method of investigating mental phenomena which in his own judgement opened up the domain of the unconscious in a way that had never been possible before; he created a method to treat neuroses and used the results of his clinical work to propose novel models of the human psyche.

For the most part, this occurred outside the university system. On the basis of his associations, he was able to build an international psychoanalytic movement with a few interested colleagues. Along the way there were false starts and blind alleys, arguments with colleagues and splits and schisms, but by the end of his life, when he died in London at the age of 83, Freud had produced a prodigious body of work and was recognized as the most famous psychologist of his era.

Freud's critics argue that the whole of his work is greater than the sum of its parts. This is not meant as praise but as a criticism of his expertise. According to his critics, Freud was a poor biologist, a sloppy clinician and an unreliable witness in his reports of his own case histories. His own followers lionized him or, if they broke from the master, recanted their previous acceptance of his theories. To this day, Freud and his psychoanalysis polarizes psychologists, patients and members of the public. Eight decades since his death, his work still has the power to shock and to challenge each new generation.

Many writers have sought to link the work of Karl Marx and Sigmund Freud.

Key Points

- With Hanns Sachs and Otto Rank, Freud founded the journal *Imago* to promote the discussion of psychoanalysis in the context of the humanities, arts and social sciences.

- In 1907, he published '"Civilized" Sexual Morality and Modern Nervous Illness', in which he argued that society could only survive if sexual instincts were repressed or their energy was channelled into socially acceptable pursuits like work and art.

- Contemporary belief was that civilizations developed from primitive forms of social organization to highly differentiated organization in industrial societies. Freud argued that psychoanalytic concepts could be used to explain the shifts of social organization.

- In *Obsessive Actions and Religious Practices*, Freud drew attention to the similarities between religious practice and obsessional neuroses.

- Treating World War I veterans led to Freud rethinking his basic theory of instincts. He grouped the sexual and ego instincts together as life instincts and contrasted them with what he called the death instincts.

Glossary

Abreaction The release of emotion caused by reliving previously repressed memories.

Ambivalence Holding contradictory feelings or impulses towards a person or object, for example, both loving and hating a parent.

Castration anxiety The male child's fear that his father will punish him for wishing to sexually possess his mother and wishing that his father would die.

Death instincts (Thanatos) The instinct to annihilate or destroy oneself.

Ego, id and superego The structural agencies that comprise Freud's second 'topography' or 'map' of the organization of the psyche.

Erogenous or erotogenic zone Part of the body that can become sexually excited.

Fixation Continued focus or regression to an earlier stage of psychosexual development.

Free association The spontaneous thoughts that Freud asked his patients to report without censorship or reservation during treatment.

Hypnosis A mental state akin to sleep, during which we are aware of our surroundings but our critical faculties are much diminished.

Hysteria Illness characterized by a wide variety of symptoms, including loss of sensations, anxiety, 'lumps in the throat', paralysis and phobias. It was originally understood as a female disease caused by a disorder of the womb. Freud offered a psychological explanation of hysteria, identifying the cause as the repression of infantile sexual wishes.

Introspection The process of trying to examine our own thought processes. According to Freud, the discovery of the unconscious and the existence of repression demonstrated that introspection was an inadequate method for psychological research.

Instinct A biological drive that seeks satisfaction. Freud offered two theories of instincts. In the first he contrasted sexual instincts (which have the goal of reproduction of the species) and ego instincts (which have the goal of the preservation of the organism). Later he contrasted the life instincts (which included the sexual and ego instincts) with an instinct towards death.

Interpretation The process by which the underlying or 'latent' meaning of actions, words, dreams and fantasies are discovered by subjecting their surface or 'manifest' meaning to the process of free association.

Libido Sexual energy that during psychosexual development is associated primarily with different erogenous zones.

Life instincts (Eros) The instincts for sexual reproduction and preservation of the individual.

Neurosis Originally neurosis meant a physical disease of the nervous system. For Freud, neurosis was a psychological disease caused by the repression of infantile sexual wishes.

Neurology Medical specialism dealing with disorders of the nervous system.

Neurone The basis structural unit of the nervous system – a cell along which nerve impulses are transmitted.

Oedipus Complex Unconscious feelings and ideas related to the wish to sexually possess the parent of the opposite sex and kill the parent of the same sex.

Pre-unconscious Mental processes of which the person having them is not aware but which are not being actively repressed.

Psychosis Disease in which the patient's understanding of reality is disturbed. Symptoms might include visual and auditory hallucinations.

Psychoanalysis A method of investigating unconscious meanings of actions, words, dreams and fantasies.

Psychosexual development Freud's account of the development of human sexuality. According to this, adult sexuality is achieved by passing through a series of phases (oral, anal, genital, latency) during which particular erogenous zones are the primary sites of sexual excitation.

Repression The process by which unacceptable impulses or ideas are made unconscious.

Resistance The opposition of the patient to the psychoanalyst's attempts to make unconscious impulses or ideas conscious.

Taboo An act against which there is an absolute prohibition – for example, incest.

Totem An object, usually an animal, which a tribe uses to symbolize their group belonging and which they venerate.

Transference The process by which patients act towards the psychoanalyst as if he or she is a figure from their past.

Unconscious Mental processes of which the person having them is unaware.

Wish fulfilment The realization of a prohibited desire in the form of a dream or fantasy.

Index

W

Y

Z

Picture Credits

t = top, b = bottom, l = left, r = right

Alamy: 107

Bridgeman Images: 37, 39

Getty Images: 37, 48, 62, 71, 75, 80, 82, 84, 126, 165r, 168, 177, 178, 222, 224, 227

J. Paul Getty Museum: 55, 58

Library of Congress: 92, 99, 110, 147

Mary Evans: 19, 171

Public Domain: 8, 23, 33, 36, 40t, 40b, 43, 51, 52, 57, 60, 65, 79, 93, 97, 103, 109, 112, 122, 129, 131, 139, 146, 149, 150, 157, 158, 159, 160, 162, 164l, 172, 180, 182, 187, 190, 191, 192, 194, 200, 202, 204, 206, 208, 214, 223, 225, 226, 230

Shutterstock: 94, 104, 134

Wellcome Collection: 13, 14, 16, 17, 24, 27, 28, 34, 41, 42, 120, 123, 133, 141, 213,